Displacement and longing for a home are not only a contemporary reality for many, but also an interweaving thread throughout the Biblical Narratives. Russell Jeung's account of his family history and diasporic calling are profoundly moving and inspiring to all Christ followers. In these stories we learn how to journey like Jesus and make sense of our own wanderings and hope for our eternal destiny.

—**Dr. Sam George,** Executive Director, Parivar International, and Co-editor of *Malayali Diaspora: From Kerala to the Ends of the World*

Russell's life long journey to live incarnationally will tug at your heart, fill your mind, and convict your soul. The story of Oak Park is a gritty life-on-life ministry that shows how a lived-out calling can bring personal discovery, multiplied disciples, and community transformation.

—**Tommy Dyo,** Strategic Partnerships and Development, Epic Movement, a Cru Ministry

I can't remember the last time that I read a memoir where I was laughing hysterically and weeping uncontrollably in back-to-back paragraphs. With much talk about justice among evangelicals these days, Russell Jeung offers the real story of an honest, embodied life of justice. If every student I have ever taught said they wanted to be the next Russell Jeung—nothing would make me more proud. Please read this book.

—**Soong-Chan Rah,** Milton B. Engebretson Professor of Church Growth and Evangelism, North Park Theological Seminary; Author of *The Next Evangelicalism* and *Prophetic Lament*

I've gotten to know Dr. Russell Jeung these past few years. I've stayed in his home. I've visited the men and women he has served. I've witnessed his sacrificial love for the Cambodian families and other refugee families in Oak Park. He is an inspiration to me and to those who know and respect him. His book about his life with Cambodian refugees reveals the strength and depth of my people.

—**Ken Kong,**

The Navigat

Russell Jeung is a rare person who embodies courage, authenticity, and integrity in a culture of consumption and assimilation. Unlike other books, *At Home in Exile* is a page turner because the author, as one of the residents, narrates the stories of Oak Park community of refugees and migrants. It is among the poor and broken, in which Jeung, a fifth-generation Hakka Chinese American, experiences the beloved community that resonates with the early Christian community under imperial Roman culture. Jeung takes the readers on his intimately courageous journey who enter into his world with a sense of belonging and ancestral roots. This is a must-read book for the homeless mind on this shore that longs to retrieve buried memories and roots for social change.

—**Rev. Young Lee Hertig, PhD,** Cofounder/Executive Director,
ISAAC/AAWOL (Institute for the Study of Asian American
Christianity)(Asian American Women On Leadership)

Many times, it is so easy to get severed from one's root and faith along the way of pursuing the American Dream in the US. It is heartening to read the life of one whom God blesses with many achievements and yet does not get disconnected from one's faith and root. I am confident that this book will inspire many others to participate more in their "exile" communities and find it at home there.

—**Kenneth VanBik, PhD,** Lecturer, Department of Linguistics
and Language Development, San Jose State University

An important biblical theme is that God speaks to His people while they are in movement, migrating or in exile. Russell Jeung invites us to recognize that we learn about God and about what God is doing when we live into our own experience of exile and choose to live and minister among migrants and exiles. *At Home in Exile* is autobiography, theology, and missiology. This book challenges us to see that exile is a unique place to serve God and to learn about how God is at work in the world.

—**Juan Francisco Martínez,** Professor of Pastoral Leadership
and Hispanic Studies, Fuller Theological Seminary

At Home in Exile is more than exploring Asian-American identity, although that certainly undergirds the story. Russell Jeung's journey is also one of deep Christian faith, committed urban life, and community activism, which together convey a compelling challenge for all followers of Jesus—namely, to embrace our ultimate identity as exiles in Christ who can speak truth to power in all cultures.

—**Al Tizon,** Executive Minister of Serve Globally, Evangelical Covenant Church

Russell Jeung's memoir of life in East Oakland is warm, humorous, and challenging. He wears his learning lightly, but it's obvious that he can teach us a thing or two about the way faith affects life.

—**Tim Stafford,** General Editor, *God's Justice: The Holy Bible*

Russell Jeung writes with great compassion, insight, clarity, and humor about his remarkable faith journey as an Asian American Christian. This book is required reading for anyone interested in race, religion, and social justice. Prepare to laugh, cry, and transform with Russell Jeung!

—**Carolyn Chen,** Associate Professor of Ethnic Studies, University of California at Berkeley

I know Russell Jeung to be a world-class academic, but he is quite unlike many scholars in that he lives out his resulting convictions in his daily life. That by itself is highly noteworthy. However, as demonstrated in this remarkable book, Jeung is also unlike the typical scholar in that he is a masterful and compelling storyteller, taking the reader not just into the daily lives of impoverished immigrants in Oakland, CA, but also inside his own struggles and transformation as he comes to identify with the poor. His talent for narrating these intermingled stories caused me to think more deeply about my own story as a grandson of immigrants from China. And as a devout Christian, it also made me question many of my own choices to avoid regularly intersecting my life with poor immigrants, especially those from parts of Asia that are in my own backyard. By showing himself to be a flawed and humble example of someone who clearly wants to follow Jesus, Jeung manages both to inspire and instruct the reader to take concrete steps in the direction of "the least of these."

—**Rev. Dr. Ken Uyeda Fong,** Executive Director, Asian American Initiative and Assistant Professor of Asian American Church Studies, Fuller Theological Seminary

Activist. Theologian. Hakka. Chinese American. Follower of Jesus. These words describe Russell Jeung and yet do not fully comprehend the story he has crafted in this masterful book. Part autobiography, part community history, and part liberation lived theology, *At Home in Exile* captures the heart and soul of following Jesus through living in community among the poor in Oakland. Follow and be transformed.

—**The Rev. Dr. Frank M. Yamada,** President,
McCormick Theological Seminary

At Home in Exile is the incredible story of a committed Christian disciple living in a poor, drug-infested, and refugee-ghetto neighborhood of Oakland, CA. As an evangelical Stanford-educated professor and a fifth-generation Chinese American, Jeung has tried to live out Jesus in this neighborhood as an exile in the US, suffering alongside refugees from Cambodia, Laos, and Burma and undocumented Hispanics. He sees the church as a mother and a home providing hope for compassion for the downtrodden, the disinherited, and the disheartened. His autobiography is truly captivating, inspiring, and moving, challenging all of us on a fundamental level to re-examine our lives of following Jesus.

—**Andrew Sung Park,** Professor of Theology
and Ethics, United Theological Seminary

In a watershed moment for refugees and immigrants, Russell Jeung felicitously reminds us of God's love for the least of these. This book powerfully illuminates the plight of the poor and disenfranchised while pointing towards the hope that is rooted and ultimately found in cruciform communities that express their faith in love.

—**Dominique Gilliard,** Board of Directors,
Christian Community Development Association

Russell's life journey is a prophetic challenge to our Evangelical affluent upward mobile suburban culture. A rarity among privileged Ivy-Leagued Asian American upbringing, his story is a must read for those who are considering a life with a purpose beyond a white picket fence in an upscale suburban neighborhood. The various lives mentioned in *At Home in Exile* fulfill a longing to see modern-day monastic examples of those who have given up the American dream for an intentional life of hardship and danger for the sake of the gospel. Written as a narrative of intriguing relationships through communal living, Russell's humor and raw wittiness is accompanied with deeper theological reflection. As a Hakka, a "guest" in exile living among refugees, Russell reminds us of the simple gospel message—that as incarnate sojourners in a broken world, we find Jesus and trust that the Kingdom is near.

—**David Ro,** Director of the Christy Wilson Center at
Gordon-Conwell Theological Seminary; East Asia
Regional Director for the Lausanne Movement

Russell Jeung's book *At Home in Exile,* at first glance, may be read as a wild adventure tale of ragtag bunch of misfits in exile, whether it be Russell—a descendant of the Hakkas, or the Cambodian refugee grandmother, or the African American gang members who stole his laptop, or the veteran who keeps waiting for his big check—all living in public housing complex. But it is so much more as he weaves the stories of their lives to lift up social injustice, racism, poverty, and obeying Jesus in a delightful storytelling!

I was inspired, challenged, and my faith and conscience pricked at times reading Russell's obedience of truly walking amongst and embracing the poor. At the same time, his transparency of his own humanness facing at times the raw reality of humanity and poverty and living in a crime-driven neighborhood makes his faith ever more real. Finally, I was inspired to want to do more as he shares the beauty, joy, life, and hope that can be found even amongst the poor and those in exile and the interconnectedness amongst all of us.

—**Hyepin Im,** President and CEO, Korean
Churches for Community Development

Jeung takes us into a decades-long journey of relocation into an urban community. He writes with the insights borne from lived experiences. Jeung writes with the acuity of a scholar, the heart of a pastor, and the soul of a Christ follower. A compelling commentary on consumerism, materialism, success, patriarchy, power, and marginality.

At Home in Exile is informed by Jeung's Asian American identity; he gives tremendous insights for people of all backgrounds. His family history takes the reader through a journey that touches on Hollywood's history, immigration history, the emergence and destruction of Chinatowns, and family and social services. It is a portrait of the unexpected way perceptions of race touch many of society's institutions—which has surprising implications for today's contentious issues.

—**Nikki Toyama-Szeto,** Director, International Justice Mission
(IJM) Institute for Biblical Justice; Author of *God of Justice*

Russell Jeung has taken elements of the Christian faith and theology, the US West Coast Asian American history/experience, life in my beloved Oakland, CA, and his own life, and woven them together in a way that is educational, engaging, and authentic. He wrestles with some of the deeper complexities of urban ministry, community justice, Christian community, life calling, and family safety in a way that gives the issues their due challenge and also gives the reader some helps on how to navigate them with intellectual and personal integrity. I highly recommend this book to anyone interested in seeing how a humble "Disney princess" has sought to be faithful to his heritage, his community, his calling, his family, and his God.

—**Rev. Phil Bowling-Dyer,** Director of Diversity
Training, InterVarsity Christian Fellowship

AT HOME IN EXILE

AT HOME IN EXILE

Meeting Jesus among My Ancestors

and Refugee Neighbors

RUSSELL JEUNG

ZONDERVAN

At Home in Exile
Copyright © 2016 by Russell Jeung

This title is also available as a Zondervan ebook.

Requests for information should be addressed to:
Zondervan, 3900 *Sparks Drive SE, Grand Rapids, Michigan 49546*

Library of Congress Cataloging-in-Publication Data

Names: Jeung, Russell, 1962- author.
Title: At home in exile : finding Jesus among my ancestors and refugee neighbors /
    Russell Jeung.
Description: Grand Rapids : Zondervan, 2016.
Identifiers: LCCN 2016015698 | ISBN 9780310527831 (softcover : alk. paper)
Subjects: LCSH: Jeung, Russell, 1962- | Christian biography—California. |
    Chinese Americans—Religion. | Evangelistic work—California—Oakland.
Classification: LCC BR1725.J48 A3 2016 | DDC 261.80973—dc23 LC record available at
    https://lccn.loc.gov/2016015698

Cover design: Darren Welch
Cover imagery: Polaris Images
Interior design: Kait Lamphere

Printed in the United States of America

16 17 18 19 20 21 /DHV/ 20 19 18 17 16 15 14 13 12 11 10 9 8 7 6 5 4 3 2 1

Contents

Foreword

I first heard about Russell Jeung from a good friend of mine when I was a junior in college. She was a few years ahead of me, and after graduating she moved to the "bad part" of Oakland to join some sort of … ministry? Faith community? Random collection of college graduates living out their Post-Adolescent Idealistic Phase? I wasn't sure.

Russell was a founding member of the ministry/faith community/ random collection of college graduates. This was about two decades ago, so I can't remember the exact words my friend used to describe him, but he came across as positively glowing.

I quietly worried that this Russell guy might be some sort of cult leader.

A few years later, my two housemates, Albert and Carl, decided to join that ministry/faith community/random collection of college graduates, which had since coalesced into a church that called themselves New Hope. I liked Albert and Carl a lot, so I went along.

We moved into a small two-bedroom unit in the building right next to the Oak Park Apartments, the informal base of operations for New Hope and the setting of much of this book.

Our building was definitely a part of the neighborhood. Our neighbors were Bosnian refugees. Our cars got broken into from time to time.

A bullet went through the window of the unit two doors down. Overall, though, the place was well-kept. The lawn was manicured, and the roof didn't leak. The landlord actually seemed to care.

Oak Park, on the other hand, was picturesque in its squalor. It looked as if a movie director had staged a set to squeeze as much sympathy as possible out of the audience. I was already writing graphic novels by then, and in one story I had a scene that took place in a rundown home, an environment meant to visually reflect the protagonist's inner brokenness. My partner on the project came to Oak Park to take reference photos.

From the graphic novel Eternal
Smile by Gene Luen Yang

Albert, Carl, and I began attending Bible studies at New Hope, and it was in this context that I finally met Russell Jeung.

Immediately, I saw that my initial concerns about him being a cult leader were unfounded. He just didn't have the charisma. Russell was a skinny Asian American guy of average height, physically unremarkable in every way. He spoke gruffly, as if he forgot to polish his words before he pushed them out of his mouth. His default facial expression was somewhere between pensiveness and disappointment.

As I got to know him, though, I realized that I was looking in the wrong place for what made Russell special.

In *At Home in Exile*, Russell again and again makes fun of his own need to be special. He compares himself to Disney princesses and mocks his childhood yearnings for a cartoon-worthy story arc. He concludes that he isn't special at all.

He's wrong, of course.

Russell lives in a way that intentionally blurs the barriers between him and his neighbors. He downplays the things that might make him stand out: his thoughtfulness, his intelligence, his multiple degrees. Instead, he takes comfort in the frailties and aspirations that we all hold in common.

Ironically, or poetically, or both, it is this utter eschewing of Specialness that makes Russell special. He listens to the Gospel's call with a rare sincerity, and he responds with decisions that are anything but common.

This book, like its author, is special. It is funny and insightful, heartfelt and challenging. It forced me to wrestle with my innermost assumptions about faith. It gave me a new lens with which to see the community around me.

This book made me pause and think and pray. It drew me closer to God.

And I believe it will do the same for you.

Gene Luen Yang
Author of comics and graphic novels

Acknowledgments

This book of "lived theology" was inspired and funded by the Virginia Seminar, part of the Project of Lived Theology. Thanks to Dr. Charles Marsh, Shea Tuttle, and the others of this group who have helped me to articulate why I do what I do.

I am grateful for a San Francisco State University Presidential Award to complete the book. SFSU College of Ethnic Studies Dean Ken Monteiro, my AAS department chairs Dr. Lorraine Dong and Dr. Grace Yoo, and fellow faculty colleagues model for me the best of Asian American Studies—that of serving and empowering the community.

Along the way, I received excellent feedback from these individuals at their institutions: Professor Karen Andrews of Westmont University; Professor David Ro of Gordon-Conwell Theological Seminary; President Frank Yamada and Professor Deborah Kapp of McCormick Theological Seminary; Professor Soong-Chan Rah of North Park Seminary; Professors Ken Fong and Daniel Lee of Fuller Theological Seminary; and Professor Grace Kao of Claremont School of Theology.

Dr. Jason Sexton's enthusiastic support made it possible for this book to come into being. I am very grateful to him and to Katya Covrett and Jim Ruark, my editors at Zondervan, whose able editing improved this text.

Various individuals have read portions of the book and encouraged me by saying they were amused by it. Thanks to Carolyn Chen, Jennifer Choo, Steve Hong, David Kim, Helen Jin Kim, Naomi Hirahara, Albert and Shauna Olson Hong, Helen Lee, Jonathan Lew, Pershing Lum, and Andrew Ong.

The Institute for the Study of Asian American Christianity (ISAAC) Book Club helped me immensely in figuring out my own theological positions. To Sabrina and Kevin Chang, Andrew and Rowena Cheung, Brian Hui, Timothy Tseng, Russell Yee, Russell Moy, Viji Nakka-Cammauf, Amos Yong, and Young Lee Hertig—I appreciate your love of learning and our discussions!

My home churches through the years—San Francisco Bible Church, Grace Fellowship Community Church, and New Hope Covenant Church—have grounded me and sustained me all my life. Harbor House should be acknowledged for being a Christian neighborhood center that served the community and introduced me to Joan. "As for the saints in the earth, they are the majestic ones in whom is all my delight" (Ps 16:3 NASB).

Oak Park Apartments will always be my home. Deeply felt thanks to Kosal Kong, Carl Williams, Veasnea Ourm, Sylvia Lopez, Keo Kong and Tane Oubkeo, Veasina Thang, and Khlot Ry who shared their stories and lives with me. They and other residents welcomed the stranger and made my life unusual and fun.

My model of Christian community will forever be shaped because of Oak Park Ministries. Those who dared to live at Oak Park and join in our unintentional community include Dan Schmitz, Rob Swift, Carlos Flores, Dan Chen, John Shou, Alice Wu (Cardona), Mae Chan (Frey), Christine Ma, Suzy Kim (Tran), Cameron Cardona, Rick Frey, and Jan Jaensen (Schmitz). Also, I am grateful for Gene Yang, who lived next door to Oak Park, for the foreword. "I thank my God every time I remember you. In all my prayers for all of you, I always pray with joy" (Phil 1:3–4).

The Chinese say, "Fallen leaves return to their roots." I am proud of my roots, that of being Hakka and Longdu, and hope that I demonstrate the noble qualities of these groups through these stories. In particular, I want everyone to see how my mother, Bernice Shue Jeung, has borne life's unexpected responsibilities with simple grace and beauty. My siblings and their families—Rod and Grace Jeung, Sandra and Stan Leong— taught me how to be family, Chinese-style, with irreverent laughter and reverent honor.

Finally, I find it somehow fitting that my own Chinese American family at home includes a Korean American of the 1.5 generation, two Chin-Burmese immigrants, and a sixth-generation American. I am very grateful that they allowed me to share their peculiarities. Bethsy and Bonny—I'm so grateful you made us your family. Matthew—you bring me ineffable, aching delight. Joan—you are God's loving-kindness to me every day and my heart's desire. I dedicate this book to you and pray that we can live out our lives as exilic guests of the King and children of God.

CHAPTER 1

Welcomed as a Guest

When I moved in with Dan Schmitz, an urban missionary in Oakland, California, I felt as if I had entered a developing country. In 1992, Oak Park Apartments was a Cambodian village in an American ghetto. Chickens ran free-range during the day but spent the nights cooped in bathrooms. Squatting, barefoot kids played with sticks in the dirt. Grandmas hung their washed sarongs alongside sausages air-drying in fly netting. Surrounding our ethnic village was an urban jungle. We lived in the Murder Dubs, the street name of the most frequently robbed neighborhood in a city known as the nation's robbery capital.

One day during the second summer I lived at Oak Park, Dan had to move out temporarily because drug dealers were threatening him. I was alone in our tiny apartment, being bitten by spiders, ants, lice, bedbugs, or some other Egyptian plague-like pest. Sitting on my mat—like our neighbors we had no beds because we hadn't enough room—I groused about the irrelevancy and obscurity of the sociological theories I was studying.

In the afternoon, I received a postcard from an ex-girlfriend. She was traveling through Bali, enjoying culinary excursions with her new fiancé. In my head, mournful violins sighed to accompany me. There I was, stuck alone in a ghetto slum, bitten by pests, surrounded by threatening drug dealers, and smugly shown up by an ex. In my self-obsession, I felt sorry for myself.

Hours later at midnight, I remained languishing in self-pity. Then came a knock on the front door. A late-night visit didn't surprise me. One time, a guy came offering me a weed-eater, something we didn't really need for our one-bedroom apartment in a concrete tenement. Another time, Dan woke up in the middle of the night to see a homeless person standing right beside him. The man had climbed through our apartment window just to borrow some more money. Oddly, another neighbor later reported that he had seen the man step through the window, but did not seem to think anything was unusual.

This time, our neighbor Orlando's smiling face appeared at the door. Orlando and his family had come from Mexico without documents and his wife took English lessons in our apartment along with some Cambodian moms. Orlando had just returned from fishing and proudly lifted his large catch for display. He generously offered all the fish to me. When I politely refused and told him to keep the fish for his family, he insisted that I take them because he didn't want to clean them.

I didn't really know what to do with the freshly caught fish, because I am used to fish that look like deep-fried sticks. So at one o'clock in the morning, I began to scale them for Orlando's family. As I thought about doing a favor for my neighbor, and as I considered how generous he had been to me, my self-pity turned to gladness and gratefulness. Once able to think beyond my own circumstances, I felt much freer.

Jesus knocked on my door that night, in the form of what some might call an "illegal alien." Orlando's generosity drew me out of my own obsessions; reciprocating his kindness further brought me outside of myself. He welcomed me into his community.

Disney Movie Dreams

I grew up on Broadway musicals and Disney movies, so I expected my life to follow roughly the same plotline. Whether the main character is Princess Elsa in *Frozen*'s Arendelle, Tarzan in the jungle, or Mulan in China, his or her family always seems to be broken in some aspect. Elsa and Tarzan are orphans, and Mulan's father is disabled.

The protagonist, who has thus won the sympathies of the audience, faces conflicts as a misfit. Princess Elsa freezes her own sister, Tarzan can't be an ape, however hard he tries, and Mulan botches trying to act like a man. They handle their identity angst by singing solos to their reflections in ice, a pool of water, or a fish pond.

In the end, however, they find fulfillment in finding their true selves and living happily ever after. Princess Elsa is saved by an act of true love, Tarzan becomes King of the Jungle and marries Jane, and Mulan saves the empire from the Huns, and the entire nation bows to her.

The plots and main characters are pretty much the same. Disney simply adds cultural touches to the movie scenes to make their summer blockbusters seem multicultural. Princess Elsa hosts dances with dukes in a towered palace, Tarzan swings with monkeys in lush forests with conveniently spaced vines, and Mulan plucks lucky crickets from her rice.

Having memorized my role as the lead in my own Disney feature film, I suffered through age-appropriate role conflicts but still expected to end up special. When I was in primary school, my mom sent me to Chinese language school for inexpensive after-school child care. I hated it, just like every other kid who had to go to Chinese school. As a fifth-generation Chinese American, I didn't even understand the instructors who taught in Cantonese.

At the time when my mother wanted me to gain some Chinese skills, the San Francisco school system wanted Chinese students to integrate into regular classrooms to make them more diverse. Since there weren't enough of my kind at Lafayette Elementary School, I had to ride a school bus to a school two miles away instead of walking two blocks to the nearest school. To my great joy, the school bus returned home too late for me to attend Chinese school, and I was able to quit.

I never did learn how to read or write Chinese, or even speak a sentence of it. Paradoxically, I was too busy being a token Chinese for the others at Lafayette and introducing them to the glories of ramen on the school's Culture Day. My mom's Rice Krispies treats would have really represented my home culture and comfort food, but that snack didn't count as authentic. Even though they were made of rice, they weren't Chinese enough, like me.

Once in high school, I continued to play the part of the cultural misfit. My friends were predominantly Asian American—Chinese, Japanese, Filipino, and Korean. None of us spoke our ancestral languages, but we did share a common, racial subculture. As urban youth, we wore black hoodies under Derby Jackets, always sat at the back of the San Francisco MUNI buses riding through the avenues on the west side of the City, and had nicely feathered, jet black hair that was split down the middle. We played street basketball day and night while listening to KSOL, at that time a radio station featuring soul music.

Even with my urban soul, I knew I wasn't black, because I felt too stiff and couldn't effect cool street gestures. I also clearly wasn't white because they were the ones who spoke out in class and I was too bored to bother, even when I knew all the answers. Being Asian American was fine on the bus in San Francisco, but once I got off the bus outside the City, I felt like Mulan trying to be either a perfect bride or a male soldier. I didn't feel comfortable in my own skin and just wanted to sing to a puddle somewhere.

Disney princesses, in the end, live happily ever after by receiving two bonuses. They stand out as heroines: unique and world-saving with their beauty, talent, and smarts. At the same time, they find belonging— accepted by their group and winning the respect, honor, and camaraderie of their peers.

I wanted the best of both worlds as well. As the youngest child in a fairly Chinese, hierarchical family, I strived to develop my own voice, one that would sing out through my abilities and accomplishments. Yet I longed for intimacy and connection with others; I hated feeling left out of anything.

Unfortunately, I do not look anything remotely like a Disney princess.

Gung Ho for Community; Produced for Consumption

My move to Oak Park Apartments in the Murder Dubs, the neighborhood of Oakland between 20th and 29th avenues, was akin to finding a treasure in a field or a pearl of great price. While I couldn't sing like a Disney princess, here I received a foretaste of the beloved community and forged a solidarity with the poor.

My grandparents and father lived in a setting similar to Oak Park. Locked out from broader society, they found refuge in San Francisco's Chinatown, where the community took care of itself with a gung ho attitude. *Gung ho*, in Chinese, means to "work together." Americans, who took note of the enthusiasm by which the Chinese worked to serve their country during the Sino-Japanese War, adopted the term to express dedication and zeal. My father, Albert, mythologized this fervent spirit of cooperation and unity, based on mutuality and social responsibility, in his own stories and endeavors. I would be enthralled by these ties among Chinese Americans that went so deep.

Yet, more than his connection to Chinatown, Dad prided himself on his independence and self-sufficiency in getting his family out of the ghetto. As he assimilated into the middle class, ethnic solidarity would be challenged by an individualistic consumer culture that conferred status by brand names instead of family names.

By dint of his hard work and industriousness, my father was one of the first in the exodus from Chinatown and the yellow middle class flight to San Francisco's Richmond District. During his off hours, he started a furniture store in Chinatown by pulling resources together with others in gung ho fashion. He and his partners named the store the

DALE Company using the first letter of all the partners' names: Dan, Albert, Lee, and Ed. My father said that they wanted to give Chinese families the opportunity to buy brand-name furniture, just like any other American in the 1960s.

Upon achieving middle class status, Albert wanted to look the part and bought the brands of that status. He always resented that, as a child, he couldn't participate in a parade with his Chinese school. Sadly, he didn't have a clean, white shirt for the occasion. Later in his life, he would never be seen in public without his Brooks Brothers suit and Johnston and Murphy wing-tip shoes. Maintaining appearances, he smoked a pipe while driving around the City in his white Lincoln Continental Town Car. The look was distinguished, but the smoke smell nauseated me as the smallest kid who had to sit in the front seat between him and my mom.

"Living in San Francisco, I have three seasons," Dad would say. "Tax season, light opera season, and football season." Having grown up during the Great Depression and enduring ostracism because of his ethnicity, he felt that he deserved to play hard after working hard. He spent the springtime working long hours of overtime to file people's taxes. Then he could relax in the summer with season tickets to Broadway musicals and in the fall with reserved seats at San Francisco 49er football games. Few would begrudge the "Greatest Generation"—those who suffered through the Great Depression, sacrificed during World War II, and developed the U.S. into a powerhouse economy—the benefits of the American way of life.

My father was himself a product of American products, aimed to create a type of consumer who didn't just purchase a product, but also a status and middle-class identity. The American economic system in the 1950s and '60s needed planned obsolescence of its products and a consumer culture of personal dissatisfaction to increase purchasing and bolster profits. By buying cars and appliances, my dad was purchasing belonging as an American.

In 1965, the U.S. opened its doors to immigration, allowing more voluntary migrants from Asia. These immigrant families, like those of the Greatest Generation, sacrificed much and went to great lengths to relocate. They were dislocated from their homes, became deaf and dumb to the language of a new environment, and often experienced downward mobility in their careers. Since they gave up so much to become Americans, logic implies that they should buy into American consumer culture or else suffer cognitive dissonance over the decision to migrate. Why else emigrate to the United States, if not to fully enjoy its financial benefits?

The American economic system and the logic of immigration into this nation-state created communities of individuals whose main affinity was their consumption pattern. Likewise, I was predestined to continue the path of upward mobility and a blessed show of status.

I would fit in if I just played my part in my community of consumption.

Awoken from the Asian American Dream

Lowell High School in San Francisco is an academic magnet school that attracts the best students in the city. From the class of 1980, my classmates included a Nobel Prize winner, a Pulitzer Prize winner, and an internationally bestselling author. My closest friends attended Harvard, Caltech, and UC Berkeley. Among the Chinese Americans, so many went on to join the top Silicon Valley tech firms that we joked about our educational and career trajectories: "Lowell, UC Berkeley, Hewlett Packard: proof there is no free will."

This was to be my fate: going to college and grad school, securing a high-paying job, and purchasing one's first property, a townhouse. Then, getting married, having kids and buying a Japanese minivan, and moving to the suburbs. Each of these steps toward being ensconced in the middle class seemed inevitable for me. My own siblings took this route. They were happy driving their kids to kung fu, piano lessons, and football practice. That would be Monday. On Tuesday, they would drive to dance rehearsals, NASA space after-school camp, and the tenth school fund-raiser of the semester.

Even in the fundamentalist church where I grew up, which warned against the dangers of worldliness, the members took upward mobility for granted. It was a sign of blessing and a witness to our families. The Asian American dream of every Tiger mom was to send her children to a prestigious university so they could build illustrious careers that would be reflected by the Lexus parked in the driveway. Then the cycle would be repeated with the next generation.

Fortunately, however, my church taught me to take God's Scripture authoritatively. When I read that the children of Israel were to have a year of Jubilee so that everyone would have land and an equal starting place, I understood that social justice was substantive, not just the right to due process. When Jesus said, "Blessed are the poor," I believed that he spoke about the materially poor, not just the poor in spirit. And when Jesus looked with compassion at the rich, young ruler and asked him to sell his possessions, I thought he was presenting that same invitation to all of us who belonged to the same community of consumption. Throughout high school and college, I often wondered about the kingdom of God that Jesus spoke of, and what it might look like here on earth.

Communist Living

After I graduated from Stanford University, I spent 1985 and '86 in Wuhan, China, teaching English. The old cadre of the group, Volunteers in Asia, ruggedly sought to live the same lifestyle as those we worked with. We slept in the same dorms as the Chinese teachers, ate at the student cafeterias, and lived on the same wages—about $27 per month. The dorms had no heating back then; it got so cold during the winter that the water on our shower floors would freeze. My Chinese friends had to instruct me how to sleep at night: by clutching a hot-water bottle and folding a down comforter around me like a foil gum wrapper. We had no hot water, either, so I avoided showering and bathing whenever I could. Luckily, since I walked around in six layers of clothing all the time, no one noticed any body odor.

I lived without television, radio, or other forms of entertainment because I couldn't understand Chinese. The majority of Chinese had little disposable income back then, so shopping or eating out weren't options to pass the time. Without these American amusements, I instead chatted with colleagues, took long bike rides at night, and read every book published in English that was available at our university.

Reflection on our collective austerity and on these books cemented my convictions and sense of calling. Along with the Bible, I found inspiration in Mao Tse-Tung's *Little Red Book* and his call for devotion to service: "Our point of departure is to serve the people wholeheartedly and never for a moment divorce ourselves from the masses . . . and to identify our responsibility to the people."[1]

This Communist ideology aligned with my parents' example of family responsibility and with Jesus' command to be a servant to all. I wept over Martin Luther King Jr.'s passion and longings in his *Letter from Birmingham Jail:* "Was not Jesus an extremist for love? So the question is not whether we will be extremists, but what kind of extremists we will be. Will we be extremists for hate or for love? Will we be extremists for the preservation of injustice or for the extension of justice?"[2]

With my fundamentalist, world-denying orientation, I felt called out of American consumption patterns. It led me to identify with the masses and become a creative extremist for love.

In addition to forming this solidarity with the poor, I came to recognize ways that the world was broken and how our lifestyles in the U.S. contribute to the severe inequities faced by the rest of the world. When my relatives welcomed me back from China, they would opine, "I bet you appreciate all the creature comforts of America, now, huh?" I would nod but held to the conviction, "Actually, I don't need all the things in America."

One other lesson from my stint in China stayed with me. Before the nation's economic liberalization, no one in China really cared much about how they looked, because they all wore the same outfits. Since there weren't many mirrors around, I would simply wake up, run my fingers through my hair to flatten it, and go to class. I had no idea how I looked and didn't really care. Apparently, none of my students did either, as they came to class with chronic bouts of bedhead. We were ugly, but were happy enough, since everyone was similarly ugly.

Then I took a short trip to Hong Kong, a capital of capitalist consumer culture. Ads blared at me wherever I went. People themselves were advertisements, as every article of clothing had its brand emblazoned on the outside. The models were Asian and resembled me, but they looked much more attractive, smart, and appealing. Mirrors were everywhere for shopper comparisons. "Ugh," I thought, "I need a haircut. My clothes are out of fashion. I need to get my teeth whitened, too . . . I suck." My life had been reduced to how I felt and looked after watching a commercial for skin products.

This sociological experiment of comparing my self-image in an advertising-saturated environment with my self-image in a controlled setting had yielded a stark contrast. When exposed to a barrage of advertising, I identified all kinds of personal shortfalls, immediately modified my behavior, purchased hair gel, and felt slightly better. Of course, if I had never left China, I would have felt just as attractive and wouldn't have had to pay $15 for Ginseng Biotin Hair Gel to add fullness and shine.

I had once seemed predestined for the suburbs, but God had other plans for me. In China, I learned that I didn't need everything that others had, and I didn't have to appear the way others looked. In the simplicity of my lifestyle, I found richness in relationships and a meaningful call. I could live without the material "blessings" that we Americans often pursue. Instead, I took Jesus literally in his critique of injustice, in his command to serve his people, and in his invitation of love. That call seemed much more irresistible than a life of washing a Lexus on a driveway in the suburbs.

A Church's Vision for the City of God

Upon returning from China, I found a church that helped me integrate my social activism and my evangelical faith. While in college, these worlds seemed opposed. My progressive activist friends would challenge, "Why do you follow the imperialistic hegemony of the white man's religion? Can't you see how Christianity has been used to colonize and exploit the world?" and I would agree. At the same time, my evangelical parachurch leaders would confront me, "Why are you wasting your time on racial politics? Don't you see how you should devote yourself to evangelism and to things eternal?" and I could see the strength of their argument.

Grace Fellowship Community Church, a church plant from the Chinese Cumberland Presbyterian Church, from the start wrestled with the question, "What does it mean to be the Church in San Francisco?" With its racial diversity, its staggering wealth inequality, and its strong views on the politics of sexual identity, San Francisco posed many questions for a group of young people wanting to be faithful in all areas of their lives. I was always impressed with what this church community could do when they joined together. One household would move to a new house, and the entire congregation would come out to help—just like an Amish barn raising. All the worldly possessions of a family of five could be moved within an hour when each church member hauled one or two boxes. We looked like frantic ants scouting a candy factory.

Supported by the church, individuals took steps of faith that were bold, especially considering their own immigrant family backgrounds and their parents' high expectations of them for upward mobility. Members relocated to the low-income neighborhoods in the Tenderloin, the Mission, and the Excelsior, and we shared a common life of intentionality and reflection. Families would invite single people to live with them, which allowed the singles to relearn healthy family dynamics and the parents to obtain childcare assistance, a huge support. Engineers quit their jobs in the defense industry because of convictions gained from our weekly Bible study. Parents enrolled their children in low-testing public schools because they believed it was more important to live faithfully in their neighborhoods than to have faith in educational attainment and financial security.

So when I wanted to move to Oak Park Apartments in the Murder Dubs, that step of faith wasn't so crazy. I had a cloud of witnesses from my own home church already doing similar, crazy things.

Welcomed and Embraced at Oak Park

In an attempt to escape my community of consumption, I discovered how the poor are blessed; I also received such blessings through solidarity with the poor. While in graduate school at UC Berkeley, I conducted a study of Southeast Asian youth, which had the largest gangs in Oakland at the time. Staff from Harbor House, a ministry in Oakland's San Antonio district, introduced me to Dan Schmitz, who had lived at Oak Park Apartments for a few years and started a cleaning business to create employment for his neighbors. He was quick to invite me to spend the summer with him. Little did he know that I would stay a decade, long enough to be legally declared his domestic partner.

Dan's apartment caused sensory overload. Boxes of food lined half of Dan's living room, since a local congregation was using Dan's apartment for their food pantry. The clutter didn't deter me, but the stench of cat pee in the carpet repulsed me. Apparently Dan's cat had never learned to use the litter box. Once I got over the reek of the wretched cat, to which I'm strongly allergic, I caught sight of the roaches. They came out in droves to throw me a welcome party. Of course, those were the bold ones; for every one out in the open, hundreds of more introverted ones stayed in the closet.

In the spirit of Christian hospitality, Dan got rid of the cat and enlisted me in his napalm warfare against the roaches. While in the dark when the roaches were unawares, we would creep up to the kitchen countertops with a lighter and Lysol spray. I would flick on the lights, and the roaches would scatter for the cabinets. Dan would be waiting with his lighter aflame and spray a fireball of Lysol at the roaches to crisp them. We spent my first night at Oak Park torching our enemies, scoring kills in video-game fashion. This night foreshadowed the many more battles Dan and I would enter in the cause of peace and justice.

The next day, the kids of Oak Park began to wander in. The Cambodian families, who lived in about half of Oak Park's fifty-six units, were close-knit, and their children were accustomed to running in and out of each other's homes. While I was at my computer, five-year-old Linda ran in and stood right beside me, peering at the screen.[3] Barefoot and wild-eyed, Linda had a mane of tousled black hair. She reminded me of the demon-possessed maniac of Gadarenes who had to be shackled, only she was a quieter, miniature version. I showed her some video games, and soon enough, she was squashed in my office chair beside me, oblivious to our tight proximity.

This was the start of the waves of kids who would come and make themselves at home in our little one-bedroom apartment. Even when we had to resort to yelling at them to go home, they would scamper to every nook and cranny, like the roaches, and never seem to leave.

The Cambodian families moved into Oak Park in the mid-'80s, resettled by refugee agencies into our neighborhood because it had the cheapest rents in the city. Twenty years after the Khmer Rouge's genocidal purge of its people, my neighbors still experienced the trauma of the Killing Fields. For a time, we held English classes in our apartment twice a week. Mostly, the classes were times for the mothers to get away from their families, have coffee, and take a break. They weren't so much English classes as they were support groups for moms.

We would practice conversations by introducing topics of everyday life. On the week when the lesson centered around TV, the moms would go around and talk about what type of programs they preferred, such as comedies, dramas, or news. Each mom around the table would share, but then one declared, "I like comedies . . . but the Khmer Rouge killed all our actors." With that, she began to sob.

This type of triggered response inevitably occurred every few weeks. Our day-to-day lives were constantly interrupted by the haunting memories of the Khmer Rouge.

Since every Cambodian adult had witnessed the execution of family members, our Oak Park community suffered from collective post-traumatic stress. The grandmas complained of nerve pains, the mothers had frequent nightmares, and the fathers gambled and drank heavily. At their ages and with their traumas, learning English and getting stable, full-time employment were out of the question. All the refugee families at Oak Park instead received government benefits.

Latinos from Mexico and Guatemala were the second-largest group at Oak Park. Felix, who lived kitty-corner to us, shared that moving to Oakland was difficult as an immigrant. He explained, "For work, I had to know where to go, where to find the streets." He wasn't talking about directions to appointments at human resources offices or to job interviews at corporations. Rather, he had to find the street corners where he could stand and have the best chance to get a casual, day laborer job. At times, he would be picked up, work all day, and still get jilted from his minimum wage pay.

Our Latino neighbors were mostly undocumented day laborers, eight men to an apartment sending remittances—gifts of money—back home. Late at night, I would hear rhythmic, constant chopping at a cutting board next door. Even in his seventies, Señor Gomez would push his fruit cart through the streets and sell papaya, mango, and elote—Mexican-style corn on the cob smeared with jalapeño mayonnaise and cheese—and then return home for another night of chopping. I like to think that my own grandfather, an illegal alien who also was a door-to-door peddler, worked with the same quiet dignity for his family as Señor Gomez.

The tenants of Oak Park were among the most marginalized in America's underclass. Our surrounding neighborhood was 52 percent Hispanic, 25 percent Asian, 16 percent African American, 3 percent white, and 1 percent Native American or Pacific Islander. One third of the families were below the poverty level and 62 percent had not completed high school.

Despite these impoverished conditions and the financial struggles of the Oak Park families, our communal life was rich with social capital: bonds of trust and reciprocity. Along with those strong social connections, we had spiritual capital: life that was intimate with God and values that sustained us through struggle. Veasina, a sweet, moonfaced child who lived with her great-grandmother, danced constantly with the same moves of those in the music videos she'd watch. She explained about the wealth of the Oak Park community: "We were all poor; we knew we were poor. But we had fun. We had ... life!"

This poor but fun, rich life showered the blessings of the kingdom on me.

Signposts for Righteousness

When Jesus said that the poor were blessed, he wasn't making a figurative comment. While I don't want to romanticize the "poor" or their environment, the economic context at Oak Park revitalized my walk with God in very concrete ways. Whereas my prayer life had become dry and Scripture reading ritualistic, living at Oak Park made these spiritual disciplines urgent for survival.

In the early '90s when I moved into Oak Park, the crack cocaine epidemic had reached its peak. Every two blocks, dealers would hail me as I drove by on East 16th Street. Initially I thought they were just being friendly, but I quickly realized that they were enthusiastic marketers for their street pharmacies. My roommate, Dan, was one of the few white people in the neighborhood, so neighbors assumed he was a crackhead on a drug run. If he got his hair cut, then they thought he was either a cop or a Mormon out of his normal uniform of a suit and tie. I, on the other hand, actually fit into the neighborhood better, as many Asian immigrants had moved into our community.

The drug dealers took up round-the-clock residence in Oak Park's parking lot, posting at our entrance and hiding their supply in car fenders or behind broken bricks in the walls of our apartments. They were so menacing that the Cambodian elders would walk a long, roundabout way to Oak Park's entrance in order avoid them. The dealers were a daily hassle, but they were part of the neighborhood scene. The crackheads who came from outside to Oak Park were much more of a pain.

Looking for a quick fix, they would steal anything. Regularly, we would find cars jacked up by bricks and the tires missing. Addicts would steal car registrations to sell to car thieves, so we scored the stickers with knives to make them hard to peel off. Frustrated, the thieves would resort to stealing our entire license plates. I even had my car battery stolen twice, so I took to using a chain and padlock to keep my car hood closed.

Outside in the streets, gangs competing for turf would mark their graffiti tags at every available spot. Our fences looked like freshmen composition drafts marked for grammar mistakes. One gang would scrawl their tag, then another gang would cross it out and sign their name. That name would then be crossed out, and the first gang would write in larger letters. I often felt like correcting their graffiti of all the grammar mistakes, such as correcting "Yous all be ho's" to "You are all whores."

Oak Park itself was graffitied, decaying, and trashed. Evicted tenants constantly dumped their mattresses and furniture in the alleys behind the apartments. Broken glass from beer bottles would be strewn across the walkways and staircases. Grass couldn't grow in the dirt patches because of the hundreds of bottle caps that were embedded in the soil. Since it was ghetto-looking, the kids didn't care about the place either, and tossed on the ground the wrappers from ice cream, chips, and elote whenever they were finished.

Just as Hong Kong billboards called out to me to buy stuff I didn't need, these visible signs of our city's brokenness spurred me to lament and pray. Before I moved to Oak Park, I knew I ought to pray but didn't feel the necessity to pray as if my life depended on it.

In East Oakland, I had constant reminders of how much my community and I desperately needed God. Sins—both society's and our own interpersonal wrongs—were pervasive, as were their consequences. One afternoon, a Cambodian boy, Phally, spat on a younger, Mexican kid, Tony, in Oak Park's courtyard. Tony complained to his parents, who came back with friends with guns. When I returned home, I heard a commotion and saw these adults shooting into the apartment of a Cambodian family. Due to a case of mistaken identity, they weren't at Phally's apartment but Lop's. Lop wasn't even involved in the earlier incident, but he had to jump out the second-floor window and escape through the back alley. Another drunken, enraged Cambodian yelled out, "They shot at my cousin! They gonna' get payback!"

Eventually, the Oakland police arrived, but they couldn't sort out who shot whom or why. They didn't have any officers who spoke Khmer, so the police left without arresting anyone, even though Tony's family had been standing in the courtyard the entire time. The next day, Lop's apartment was emptied. Fearing for their lives, the family moved to Fresno overnight.

In Oakland, a minor confrontation between boys escalates into shootings and gangs looking for even more retaliation. This tragic cycle of violence victimizes the combatants, innocent bystanders, and their families. Mistakes about racial identity and barriers of language exacerbate such situations, while institutions such as the police prove ill-equipped to handle them. This institutional failure exemplifies the broken nature of the systems in our society, that is, the structural sins of inequality and racism. Lop had no business in Phally's and Tony's conflict, but he bore the brunt of its repercussions.

These regular dramas of the underclass impelled me to cry out daily, "Thy kingdom come, thy will be done." I yearned—and still do—so much for God to make things right. People sometimes say that Alcoholics Anonymous meetings are how church services should really run. The members attend, recognizing their desperate, utter reliance on God and others. The first step of their twelve steps is to declare, "We admitted we are powerless over alcohol—that our lives had become unmanageable."

Living in the Murder Dubs, I could easily admit that we were powerless over sin—that our lives in this community were unmanageable and lamentable. While the same is true in middle-class neighborhoods, our depravity there is not as readily recognized. Street scenes of Oakland were icons calling me into God's sacred presence. They were signposts, reminding me to seek first God and his righteousness.

Quickened to God's Voice

Not only did relocation into the inner city press me toward God, but it made God's words more distinct and clear to me. I had grown up with daily quiet times, but reading the Bible had become a legalistic chore and required interpretive stretches to relate its passages to my circumstances. Although I moved only fifteen miles from San Francisco to Oakland, I entered a setting in Oak Park where the Bible immediately and directly addressed my situation.

Favorite passages of God's promises, such as Jeremiah 29:11, became more plainly understood. Before, when I read that God declares, "For I know the plans I have for you, plans to prosper you and not to harm you, plans to give you hope and a future," I thought that God had a nice career in mind just for me. When considering my neighbors at Oak Park, I realized how small my self-preoccupation was. This passage—written to a whole nation and not just to a guy wanting a Disney fairy tale ending—offers so much more promise, especially to low-income immigrants and refugees. Here God is pledging to fulfill the deepest longings of whole groups of exiles; to return from banishment and shame to be reunited at home, at peace and liberated.

Other passages, which once seemed so foreign or metaphorical, now related to the concrete conditions in which I found myself. At Grace Fellowship, we sang a song based on Psalm 91: "You will not fear the terror of night, nor the arrow that flies by day.... A thousand may fall at your side, ten thousand at your right hand, but it will not come near you." For the American middle class, these arrows might represent sharp words from a supervisor or a family member, whom one grimly endures.

For us at Oak Park, these arrows were actual bullets. Indeed, during the two decades I have lived in Oakland, more than 2,000 individuals have been shot and killed, including children who were innocent bystanders. My own home has been shot at twice, and a bullet hole through our dining room window reminds us of the terror of night. Arrows that fly by do not allude to intangible perils, but represent very present dangers requiring our utmost trust in God. So it is with those living in war zones where refugees must flee or in areas of organized crime in which parents send off their children unaccompanied.

As I read the Bible at Oak Park, I realized that many of God's words, though offered to all, were directed to the poor and for the poor. The favorite story about Jesus for many kids at Oak Park was his feeding of the 5,000. They found it miraculous that Jesus had transformed the hardened, selfish hearts of many people to share what they had. With faith in God's economics of abundance, the youth assumed that the world has enough for all; unfortunately, some people, including Jesus' disciples, see only what they don't have.[4]

As I read Scriptures through the eyes of those around me—refugees and aliens—God spoke loudly to me his words of hope and truth. Blessed are those who are poor, for they cry out for his kingdom to come and heed his words of promise. While these interpretations may be prosaic or already evident, they helped me understand how God so loved the world. In the affluence and might of the United States, I found it easy to relate to the power of Jesus' resurrection, just as Paul prayed about his sole purpose to know Jesus. At Oak Park, though, I came to fellowship with Jesus' suffering as I lived alongside the poor.

Open Spaces of Embrace

Recognizing the poverty of our human condition created space for an Oak Park ethos of hospitality and mutuality. As a newcomer to Oak Park, I was surprised at how quickly I was embraced by an entire village, both old and young. Even across cultural distance and language barriers, the residents opened their homes and their hearts to me. This welcome might have been based on traditional obligation or the children's need for attention, but nonetheless the generosity of their time and resources touched this equally attention-seeking student.

Like everyone in the Jeung family, I have great fun with kids. At Oak Park, they spilled out everywhere—in the trees, on the rooftop, in the parking lot, and mostly, in the complex's huge courtyard. Since their parents often were unemployed and stayed at home singing karaoke or gambling, the kids would be driven outside and left to their own devices. They'd scamper across the courtyard in small herds. Often bored, they would barge into our apartment looking for anything to do.

For my own amusement and as procrastination from my studies, I would see what I could get the kids to do. I was aghast at how much they spent on junk food, since Coke and Flaming Hot Cheetos bought from the corner store seemed to be the daily breakfast for most. The youth and I initiated microenterprises to recycle neighborhood dollars instead of their being sent to transnational snack corporations. We alternated between making brownies, Jell-O, cupcakes, and Rice Krispies treats to sell to others in the complex. I told the Cambodian and Latino children that Rice Krispies treats are a traditional Chinese snack, and they were suitably appreciative of the cross-cultural experience. After the initial capital outlay was repaid, the sellers for that day would keep their profits.

Baking was fun for the youth, since the ovens in their apartments typically were used only as storage spaces for pots and pans. Marketing and selling, though, were the most exciting aspects of our venture, as the kids had to find two dozen customers to sell all their stock. They put up a sign in our window, "We Take Food Stamps," and would also go door-to-door peddling their merchandise. Later, I introduced the concept of tithing, and the kids put 10 percent of their earnings into a casserole pot guarded by a stuffed bunny and labeled "God's money." That money would then be spent—by majority vote—on where to go to eat together.

What I found so amusingly random—making my ethnic snack Rice Krispies treats, accepting food stamps for homemade baked goods, and tithing via a rabbit usher—became the afternoon norm for Oak Park kids. I enjoyed the absurdity because it reflected our unlikely community. I grew up skiing at Lake Tahoe; no one in the apartments around me had ever seen snow. I had met heads of state; the refugees and undocumented neighbors were stateless. Soon after I moved into Oak Park, other Christians from UC Berkeley joined us there to seek Jesus among the poor, and despite our vast differences, we became a tight community through our shared life. That life together was intense and full even when much of what we did cost nothing.

Rob Swift, who was getting his master's in teaching English as a second language at the time, also moved into Oak Park from his hometown in Silicon Valley. During the summers, we would drive to the beach at nearby Alameda, and the kids we brought along would immediately run into the water, even with all their clothes on. He and I would watch the kids play in the California sun, sit back in our lawn chairs, and sigh knowingly to ourselves, "It's rough doing urban ministry."

After a day in the water—strangely, storm drains spilled out right onto the beach—the kids would return to Oak Park to enjoy "bagel dogs," that is, hot dogs wrapped in bagels that were leftovers from the factory. One earnest boy, Samath, said he took a shower after eating a few bagel dogs, and then promptly threw up. Out of all the things that could have made him sick—getting dehydrated at the beach, splashing around in drainage water, chasing other kids all day, and eating old, processed meat by-products—he deduced, "I'm not going to take baths anymore." Employing similar logic, we Christians at Oak Park found great joy in our impoverished circumstances: we weren't so satisfied with our middle-class status in the first place, so we don't really need money.

For no-cost lunches, we would go to Costco and enjoy their samples. Once, the sample lady asked our bedraggled group of Cambodian and Latino children where their parents were. Maria, one of the Latina girls, pointed to me, the Chinese guy. When the lady eyed the seven of us quizzically, Maria answered, "You should see the rest of us at home!" and we promptly headed to the next food stand.

Our abundant life was free, and we had each other.

In my darkest moments, when kids were shot or our apartment burglarized, the kids were my solace. I recall feeling morose one grey, wintry day and taking some children to a redwood forest nearby. As we hiked, the girls linked arms with me and chatted about nothing in particular. Suddenly, we came across clumps of ladybugs—tens of thousands of them swarming. We stood transfixed, gaping at the colony's red brilliance against a log. It was my burning bush, informing me that we were in sacred space. To this day, I cannot recall what made me depressed. But I won't forget how God's beauty shook me from my self-focus, or how his children led me there by the hand.

Alice Wu-Cardona, one of the UC Berkeley alumni who studied city planning while living at Oak Park, recalled how the children enthusiastically showered her with love. On her first birthday while at Oak Park, the children poured into her apartment and excitedly handed her a bag full of goldfish. What could she do? She felt obligated to drive to the pet store and purchase the requisite tank, filter, gravel, and chlorinating drops. Although only two fish survived, Alice recounts that they remained with her the entire five years she lived at Oak Park. She later reminisced, "Their bulging eyes and gulping mouths were constant reminders of the kids' enthusiastic, not-thought-through, no-holding-back love. I think I need to love more like this, just a little more like this." Unabashed children, swarming ladybugs, and long-lasting goldfish. Even in the inner city, we received God's warm embrace.

The grandparents of Oak Park were also gracious hosts who took us bumbling college grad students into their homes. After losing her husband and four sons to the Khmer Rouge, Khlot Ry survived their reeducation camps and escaped with her granddaughters to the Thai border. She was first resettled in Utah, but later moved to Oakland to be close to other relatives.

In her eighties, Khlot Ry sold candy and bagel dogs to the children of the complex for extra income. I often took her to Costco, when I didn't have a group of kids with me, to help her purchase a stock of candies, bagel dogs, and popsicles. Over time, I could understand her limited English vocabulary. She'd ask, "Bags—small, small?" and I would retrieve some snack-sized ziplock bags for her. Still, she would mock me for failing to learn any Khmer: "Russell, you live Oak Park five years. Why you no speak?" and then she'd cackle with the other grandmas along for the ride to Costco.

To American outsiders looking at her, Khlot Ry was a poor refugee who had to sell candy on the side while living in a slum. Yet when she returned to Cambodia for a visit, she was a returning dignitary. Her nephew was the government's Minister of Labor. Even King Norodom Sihanouk and Queen Norodom Monineath personally met with her for her service to the Buddhist community when she brought donations to the villages.

Whenever I stopped by, Khlot Ry gave me a royal welcome, served me a drink, and asked "Nam bai?" meaning, "Have you eaten rice?" Then she'd feed me whatever she had, which was usually bagel dogs. When I introduced Joan, my wife-to-be, to her, Khlot Ry shook my shoulders and announced proudly and repeatedly to Joan, "Russell, like my son." For a wedding gift, Khlot Ry gave Joan a huge gold band.

Such Khmer hospitality—assuming others' wants, serving refreshments, preparing a meal, sitting together for hours, and sharing generously, even with little to spare—was not just an ethnic form of politeness, but invitations to relationship and love. By feeding me, Khlot Ry welcomed me to her table and into her family. At her home, she attended to my physical well-being and my soul. Within her family, she regarded me with both affection and expectation, with pride and acceptance.

Orlando was Jesus, as an illegal alien, knocking at my door. Khlot Ry was also Jesus, as a frail refugee, welcoming me to his banquet.

Recently, Khlot Ry passed away. When I went to pay my respects, Veasina, her great-granddaughter, handed me a bottle of water, laid her hand on my shoulder, and gently shared, "Grandma would've wanted you to have this." At that, I broke down.

You see, Asians demonstrate their love through food. Khlot Ry didn't have to hug me or verbalize her love for me; instead, she fed me with her abiding concern and provisional care. Likewise, when Veasina handed me the water, she was pouring out love—that of her grandmother and her own—during this time of grief.

When I was a stranger and new to Oakland, the Oak Park children and grandmothers invited me in. When I was hungry, they fed me bagel dogs. When I was thirsty, they offered me drink. For twenty years, this community of refugees took this privileged, wandering guy into their family and embraced me. Although I was used to earning what I got, here I didn't have to do a thing.

Mutuality of Need, Mutuality of Support

Like individuals in Alcoholics Anonymous, we at Oak Park acknowledged our neediness and brokenness. Asking for help and relying on one another, then, were also common community practices. As described earlier, our front window and door were knocked upon incessantly. Located on the ground level, our apartment became the kids' convenience station, good for pit stops and fill-ups. Like many of the knocks, again Jesus was calling on me.

This afternoon, Ray came a-knockin'. Ray was one of the three white people living in our complex, yet he fit into our landscape just right. A grizzled, unkempt alcoholic, he would often be seen with his usual Budweiser in hand. This day, however, he carried an electric hair trimmer.

"Russell, can you shave my head?" Ray slurred.

I was instantly repulsed by the thought of touching Ray, let alone running my fingers through his hair. I also didn't want to have to hear again his far-fetched delusions, that soon his "check would come in the mail," and then he would marry a beautiful Cambodian bride and help our neighbors buy more beer.

Because he wore military fatigues, I assumed for some time that he was a spaced-out Vietnam War veteran, a bit older than Dan and I. I later found out he was only in his late twenties. The drinking, smoking, and heavy diet of bagel dogs certainly had worn on him.

"Uh, why me? Can't you get someone else to do it? I'm busy right now," I claimed. This last statement was extremely ironic, because as a graduate student I was rarely busy; I would do anything to procrastinate, such as copyedit graffiti, drive kids to the beach, or take grandmas to Costco. I even cleaned a neighbor's apartment, including the area behind the refrigerator, to put off writing. But I didn't want to touch Ray's head.

"C'mon, you can do it. I even have the razor!" He proudly lifted it up for my viewing.

"I don't think so. I can't cut hair," and so I excused myself and returned to my hypothetical work. However, the popular evangelical acronym at the time, as seen fashionably on wristbands, kept nagging at me: "WWJD?—What would Jesus do?"

A little later, another knock came at my door, this time at the usual three-foot height. "Are you gonna' cut Ray's hair?" Dana squeaked. "He's waiting now." I had been wrestling with what to do, but the hopeful request from my little neighbor won me over. Who would want to let down a poor, bored child whose excitement for the day was to view the carnage of a bad haircut? Together, we marched three doors over to Ray's apartment.

Ray was in the kitchen, smiling serenely like the Buddhist monks who came yearly to Oak Park for offerings. His cupboards were bare except for the roaches brazenly scouring the walls and avoiding our nightly torchings. I tried to breathe through my mouth because the place smelled of acrid cigarette smoke, which Dana didn't seem to notice, intent as he was to witness the landmark shearing.

I turned on the trimmer, pressed it against Ray's pasty white scalp, and mowed the first swatch of hair. "This isn't too bad," I thought, as I avoided making skin contact with his head. I proceeded with gusto, and within minutes I had cropped all his hair. Ray ran his hand over head from front to back and side to side.

"Smooth, Russell, smooth. Wanna' beer?" he intoned.

"No, thanks. I'm good."

And I felt good, especially after going home, washing my hands, and using hand sanitizer. Then repeat. Jesus commands us to love our neighbor and the body of Christ with gung ho spirit, but that's often hard to do when our neighbors are self-sufficient, spaced evenly apart in suburban tract homes and occupied with maintaining all their stuff. It's even difficult in our postmodern churches, where congregations primarily cater to the needs of individuals.

But at Oak Park, loving my neighbors was easy because they came knocking all the time. Whether children or adults, they were not ashamed to seek help. Although I treated Ray as an untouchable, he enlisted himself in my community. Fortunately, our community also included kids like Dana, who prodded me with their enthusiasm. In Cambodian culture, one's head is sacred, so to pat someone is a grave sign of disrespect. Ray, on the other hand, invited me to love him as a neighbor so that touching his hair became a sacred act of worship and fellowship.

Unintentionally, Ray helped us build an intentional community. In the end, he really did receive his big check from the government, and he bought furniture for a few families. He even journeyed to Cambodia to bring back a beautiful bride, much to everyone's surprise. Although he has passed away, I still think about Ray and how gung ho he was to get his head shaved. Given the choice, cutting the hair of someone like Ray would still not be at the top of my list of pleasurable things to do. But sometimes, in a community with a Dana and a Ray, one has no real choice. We needed each other, and we needed to be there for one another.

An Intervention from Roach

Whenever I needed my neighbors, they were there for me as well. Once, someone stole my laptop from our apartment. As a budding scholar, all I knew was on that hard drive; I certainly didn't keep anything in my head. Aggravated by my lost work, I was even more incensed that I knew who had stolen my computer. A runner for one of the dealers out front had grabbed it. My lower back muscles tightened in knots as I stressed over the near presence of my "enemies." We had begun our organizing efforts to drive out the dealers, who responded by slashing our tires, threatening us, and now stealing our possessions. Like the psalmist, I felt surrounded by those who hated us.

According to our on-site manager, who knew the dealers, word on the street was that I could buy back my laptop. I was excited, since for me getting "word on the street" was the closest I could get to hearing a word of knowledge from the Holy Spirit. He said that I should pay a visit to Roach.

Roach, who lived on our side of Oak Park, roomed with George, a 300-pound man who had been convicted of manslaughter. Roach told me on the down low that I could retrieve my computer for $100.

Wanting to catch my enemy, I reported this information to the Oakland Police Department. They said I should arrange a meeting time, and then they would wiretap me under my clothes. I could obtain a verbal confession from the thief, and then they would swoop in for the arrest.

As this was the stuff of television cop shows, I was all in. I arranged a meeting time and place with Roach and got my cash payment in mint condition, small denominations. Then I contacted the sergeant of OPD Robbery Division, reporting that the "eagle has almost landed."

The sergeant checked, and then informed me that the electronics technician was away on vacation. "Jeez," I thought, "no wonder no one ever calls the police." After I complained that I had spent all this time setting up a deal with a fence, he advised that I should pay and at least get back my computer.

Dejected, I felt even more idiotic once I realized that I was going to meet with a guy named Roach. Who lived with a huge convicted murderer. In the middle of the night in the hood. With all straight up cash. Now I was the setup.

Fortunately, I knew—through word on the street—that everyone at Oak Park seemed to own guns. I asked Kosal, who lived upstairs, to watch my back from his bedroom window overlooking the parking lot as I went to pay Roach. Kosal had come to Oak Park a decade earlier to live with his ten relatives in a one-bedroom. A soldier in the Cambodian Civil War, he lost his fiancée during the Killing Fields, but survived and eventually made it to Oakland. He was accustomed to having a gun and using it.

Unfortunately, Kosal didn't fully understand me when I asked him to be my backup. Instead, he conscripted another Cambodian guy, and they walked out into the darkness to join me. I headed out in the lead, my posse marching behind in grim determination. If you saw us in a movie, we'd be walking in slow motion in formation, with ominous music crescendoing to confront the dangerous villains.

Doing the gangster lean against my car, Roach simply told me that my computer had already been fenced.

Rats! My live-action crime drama ended abruptly.

I never did get my computer or catch the thief, but I did receive something more—the backup of my neighbors, including Roach.

Just as gangs need numbers for physical protection, especially when police staffing is inadequate to provide security, we needed our neighbors for help in time of need. Being where we were, the time of need was always the present.

From a Community of Consumption to Solidarity with the Poor

My father grew up in a wonderful, close-knit environment, but escaping poverty and gaining middle-class status made too much sense to pass up. In American meritocratic fashion, he believed he deserved all that he had earned. Similarly, surrounded by advertising that has a cultural monopoly of space, I had come to feel that only through consumption could I be satisfied, or at least, could I look good. As social animals who compare ourselves to one another, we often unintentionally adopt the busy schedules and spending patterns of those around us. Our freedom for the pursuit of happiness in the United States, consequently, now enslaves us.

Our market-driven sensibility pervades even church discourse, as I often see individuals church-shopping to find a place that meets their needs and where they can belong. One's church community is often based on what Robert Bellah and coauthors term affinity groups in "lifestyle enclaves."[5] We find fellowship among others who are most like ourselves, who share our economic lifestyle and personal interests.

Even church small groups, where American Christians can develop their most intimate fellowship with one another, tend to assume a type of community based on a market exchange model. Rational individuals invest their time and psychic energies. In return, they receive emotional support, prayers for their issues and circumstances, and most significantly, a Spirit-led sense of belonging as God's people. When these transactions aren't fully met, however, the social contracts among individuals may break down. Often, Christians base their understandings of community from therapeutic models; they understand "true community," as opposed to pseudo-community, as a state where members are contemplative and self-aware, safe and vulnerable, free and non-hierarchical.[6] In this ideal type, individuals give of themselves to construct a spirit of community.

On the other hand, Chinese gung ho solidarity differs from such communities of consumption, Disney creations of belonging, and even the Christian models of community based on therapy. Rather than a group of individuals coming together on their own terms, solidarity starts with the collective as one's extended family. Members think of themselves as family first and foremost. The group is not made up of rational individuals, but of persons who cannot survive without one another. Individuals don't seek what they can get out of the group, but instead look to how they can contribute to the group's overall health and well-being.

Christian solidarity with the poor is similar to this gung ho mentality in our acknowledgment of our common humanity and neediness. Our unity is not based on our humanly constructed connections, but on the Spirit's life in us and through us as the body of Christ. We are already the community of God; we simply need to examine ourselves to see if we are living out this unity.[7] As stated in Paul's letter to the Ephesians, we are fellow citizens with God's people and members of his household.

How can middle-class Americans, especially those of us in the suburbs, attain this solidarity with the poor? It's difficult, when middle-class persons like myself are continually complicit in the oppression of the poor, as the food we eat and clothes we wear often are produced by exploited labor. We avoid poverty, as only 10 percent of Americans see themselves in the lower class despite the steep decline of those with middle-class earnings. Within our communities of consumption, our narrowed self-interests and harried lifestyles keep us from lamenting and from doing justice. Instead, we contribute to the sufferings of others by our indifference.

Part of my repentance, then, is to identify with the struggle of the poor. I do so by reclaiming my Chinese heritage and appreciating the sacrifices of my ancestors in China and in America. By living among those in low-income communities, I have come to see the pernicious effects of structural injustice and inequities on their lives. And by longing for God's kingdom of peace to come and by hearing his Word spoken to the poor, I develop this solidarity.

Through unity with the poor—by admitting that not many of us "are influential, not many are of noble birth" (1 Cor. 1:26) and in continuing to "remember the poor" (Gal. 2:10)—we gain the blessings of the poor. At Oak Park, I have received the free embrace of children and that gives me a concrete glimpse of Jesus' unconditional pleasure in me. I have been warmed by the gracious hospitality of elders, who have shown me the Father's lavish mindfulness of me.

In solidarity with the poor, we further develop a sense of our humanity and our fellowship with the saints. We become more heavily burdened by the fact that nearly half of us live on less than $2 a day and that our environment is quickly being devastated. Knowing that we'll spend eternity with our brothers and sisters in Christ from the Global South, where two thirds of Christians now live and are mostly poor, we work towards faithful lives that are pure and faultless and "look after orphans and widows in their distress" (James 1:27).

Oak Park brought me into solidarity with the poor. Our unlikely community was not necessarily an intentional Christian community, but it was one that was clearly unified by the Spirit. One night, Kosal helped Dan and me clean up the glass after a thief smashed my car window to get change. Upon receiving our gratefulness, he didn't comment on our common victimhood or our shared individual interests. Rather, he simply stated our taken-for-granted support for one another and unity: "That's okay. We're all in this together."

CHAPTER 2

Ancestral Choices

When my son Matthew was in preschool, he played a game of musical chairs with his Sunday school class. In this version of the game, the one left standing when the music stopped was the winner, and the prize was getting to tell the group what made him or her special.

Round after round, a little student would win, state their name, and then share their unique attributes.

"I'm Sierra, and I'm special because I'm wearing Hello Kitty socks."

"I'm Peter, and I'm special because I can dance the hula."

Finally, Matthew won but he didn't appear too pleased. "Come on, Matthew! Tell us your name and how special you are!" urged the Sunday school teacher. Matthew looked down and shook his head.

"God made you just who you are! Tell us how special you've been made!" the teacher offered in positive reinforcement.

Matthew again made his grumpy face by scrunching up his nose. In reality, he didn't want to win and leave the game, but wanted to continue playing.

"You are unique! Share with us what makes you, you!" prodded the teacher.

Finally, in an outburst of toddler exasperation, Matthew yelled, "I'm

NOT special!" He promptly sat back down—just an average kid—with the rest of the other losers.

The Cult of Specialness

As I wrote previously, I have narcissistic, Disney-like self-expectations—to be accepted by the group, as well as to stand out from the crowd.

In this country, each of us is special. We are supposed to develop healthy self-esteem from our unique gifts and talents. We are to take pride in our ethnic culture and value our diversity. Once firmly established in our identity and grounded in our roots, we can flourish as fully actualized human beings. We develop our individual ideas and personalities, make our own decisions, and live independently.

That is, unless you have to move back with your parents because the costs of living are too high.

Americans seem to see themselves as cells in mitosis. They slowly separate from their parent cells in phases. In "healthy" stages of child development, children must work through issues like toilet training to become autonomous or like schoolwork to develop initiative and self-esteem. Better to let your kid become toilet trained when he is ready, lest he become anal retentive with an undue sense of shame. After all, there's nothing embarrassing about wearing size 8XL Pampers diapers.

Similarly, American Christians have long adopted the self-esteem movement, almost to the point of reducing the faith to a utilitarian means to self-fulfillment and personal growth. Since the 1980s American Christianity has seen an increasingly individualistic orientation toward privatized faith. More recently, greater numbers of Americans have sought authenticity in their faith and chafed against institutionalized forms of religion as too hypocritical and judgmental. The rise of individualism, as exemplified by "spiritual, but not religious" persons, relegates faith into one's inner life, primarily for one's own interest.

One example of this American Christian evangelical focus on the individual is found in the "best-selling nonfiction hardback in history,"

The Purpose Driven Life.[1] In his book, megachurch pastor Rick Warren suggests how an individual might find one's purpose. After he recognizes that we were formed for God's pleasure and for his family, Warren goes on to help individuals find their unique roles in life. He recommends that, "You will be your most effective when you use your spiritual gifts and abilities in the area of your heart's desire, and in a way that best expresses your personality and experiences. The better the fit, the more successful you will be."[2]

Another example of being special in the United States is the discourse on multiculturalism. To combat the feelings of marginalization such as I felt as a young Chinese American, today's youth are taught to take pride in their cultural heritage and to recognize that diversity is beautiful. People of color may continue to face segregation, discrimination, and racial profiling, but at least we can be represented in billboards and be accepted as consumer markets!

I felt slightly proud about being Chinese in the United States, because I was different and unique. But then I thought about it. There are about 1.4 billion Chinese in the world. What's so special about being one of out of every five humans on earth? Perhaps I stood out because I was Chinese American, an overseas Chinese. Yet that's not a unique status, either. There are 47 million others just like me. That's not special Disney material at all.

Hakka Royalty?

Luckily, I knew that in my blood I am Hakka, a distinct linguistic group in China. That might differentiate me from the crowds of Chinese on the bus. That would certainly alleviate the marginality of not being black or white in America.

While growing up, I scarcely knew what it meant to be Hakka. My father proudly relayed to me that the Hakka were "rebels, nomads, and pirates." I tried to picture myself in these occupations, but those job skill-sets didn't seem very marketable in San Francisco in the 1980s.

So when I had a free afternoon while traveling in Hong Kong in

2009, I went in search of my roots in the Tsuen Wan district. There, I hoped to find clues about my Hakka heritage. Perhaps they would have cool styles of art or music. Maybe I could find records of my ancestors, and trace my lineage back for centuries. I longed to locate a metaphorical home where I could hang my hat, or better yet, a princely crown. I could be the descendant of a Hakka king, for all I knew.

Once a sleepy fishing village that was a homogenous ethnic enclave, Tsuen Wan had since replaced all traces of previous Hakka presence with towering residential blocks and neon shopping malls. Despite this urban sprawl, Tsuen Wan hosted one remaining Hakka remnant—the Sam Tung Uk Museum, a Hakka walled village with twelve original houses.

With much anticipation, I took the subway there from my hotel and approached the blank, white-washed walls of the museum. They were windowless and without ornamentation, built as a defense from pirates of the Pearl Delta. Before I entered its wooden gates, I paused to collect myself. My own forebears may have once trod the hallowed halls of Sam Tung Uk ("three rows of dwelling").

I took a step into my past, but quickly discovered only hollow echoes. The hallway was unadorned of art or decoration. I expected to enter more interesting exhibits in the other spaces, yet the inner rooms were quite barren, too. The living room had a wooden bench and a small shrine, but no specific lattice work, no exquisite pottery, not even decorative flooring.

I became increasingly dismayed as the bedrooms and a closet containing typical Hakka clothing further revealed the simplicity of my people. Shirts and pants were made of black cloth without any embroidery or coloring. Only the hats were distinctive for their curtain fringes used to keep out the sun.

I was getting disappointed about the Hakka culture; I expected a little more from a minority group that had been distinct for over twenty-two centuries. Then I came upon the kitchen. "Ah, now I will see how we make our mark," I thought to myself. "Chinese live to eat, so Hakka cuisine must have some fine delicacies."

At this interactive museum exhibit, woks with bamboo steamers sat atop brick stoves. I lifted the steamer lid and readied myself to discover some scrumptious-looking Hakka treat.

Chicken Crap Dumplings.

The signature Hakka food was named "Chicken Crap Dumplings"! Ha, that must have been one of those placards that lost something in translation from Chinese to English. Earlier on that trip, we had come across a sign with a picture of slithering reptile. It alerted: "Warning! Snacks may bite!" We quickly scanned our surroundings for dangerous Rice Krispies treats.

As I read further, I was disappointed to learn that the dish was labeled correctly. The Hakka chicken crap dumplings were tea cakes made of glutinous rice and small black seeds. The seeds looked like chicken crap.

Was this the apex of Hakka culture and civilization? There had to be something more inspiring about my people; how else could I feel special about my family and myself?

Roots at the Chinese Village of Point Alones

When I returned from that trip to Tsuen Wan and researched a little further, I learned that my people were not simply modest and unassuming. They were also despised.

My people have no name for themselves. The term *Hakka* literally means "the guest families." We have moved so often that we don't know where we originally started. As the guests of other Chinese for millennia, we have no identity save our subordination to others.

One missionary wrote about the Hakka's stigmatized, underclass status in China during the mid-nineteenth century: "If you were to ask a thoroughbred Punti (original landowners) about the character of the Hakkas, he would certainly, in the case of his condescending to acknowledge that he ever heard of such people, turn up his nose and tell you that the Hakkas are quite beneath your notice, that they are a kind of semi-barbarians, living in poverty and filth."[3]

Given their lowly reputation, the Hakka in China have been dispossessed and forced to migrate multiple times since the Jin dynasty (265–460). Name the barbarians. We've been driven out by them—by Huns, Manchus, and provincial warlords. Since we had to move so much, our women knew better than to bind their feet.

The Hakka led the massive Taiping Rebellion against the Chinese emperor (1850–64) and engaged in the Punti-Hakka Clan Wars in Guangdong Province (1855–67), but they lost both times. In retreat, the group was driven literally to the edge of China. Some even faced forced resettlement onto a reservation in the subprefecture of Chiqi.

At that time, when she was only eleven years old, my great-grandmother Hall Gock Tie found herself about to join the Hakka diaspora, too.

Without any land to farm or waters to fish, her father and mother led Gock Tie and her two brothers on another Hakka migration in 1868 that would take them even farther than those who journeyed to Southeast Asia. They were lured to California—the Gold Mountain.

Gock Tie must have clearly remembered the day they left Hong Kong to pioneer a whole new life for themselves. Fifty-five years later when she testified to her son's birth on U.S. soil, she easily answered the U.S. immigration officials who probed about the year of her arrival. In 1868, the overwhelming majority of Chinese migrants from Hong Kong were men. Hoping to get wealthy in California and then return, only one out of three eventually made it back to Guangdong. The rest, we surmise, remained stranded in a hostile land with just the company of their brothers.

But Ah Hall, my great-great-grandfather, was not a sojourner. Since he had no land for his family to tend, he could not leave them behind to take care of themselves and the family gravesites. Instead, he paid over $1,000 to secure passage on a steamship for his entire family. In exchange for borrowing that steep amount, he owed three full years of work to the foreign brokers.

Through Hakka family connections, Ah Hall heard that a Chinese family accustomed to fishing at sea could make a home at Point Alones. Set in a cove across from where the Monterey Bay Aquarium now sits, Point Alones was ideal. The bay teemed with seafood, and the beach was a mile away from town, far from the stern white townspeople.

This Chinese immigrant village differed greatly from the Chinese urban settlements, mining camps, or even other fishing villages in California. It featured women and children. The demographics were unusual because the Chinese normally could afford to send only men to be laborers. Further, in 1875 the U.S. Congress passed the Page Act, which aimed to "end the danger of cheap Chinese labor and immoral Chinese women"; immigration of Chinese women virtually stopped. Yet at Point Alones, twenty of the forty-seven Chinese there in 1870 were women, and fifteen were "small specimens of the Mongol type," as the local newspaper described the children.

Although a small specimen, Gock Tie went to work alongside her parents right away. Yankee hunters had decimated the otter population in Monterey for their fur by the 1850s, leaving the abalone population to explode. The Chinese arrived right at that time, and set up a fishing camp. Ah Hall and the men would pry the abalone off the rocks, while Gock Tie and her mother would shuck, clean, and dry the meat at the beach. Huge shell mounds were left scattered throughout the beach.[4]

To their surprise, the Chinese later found that the shells of the abalone were valuable to the strange white devils, as they called Anglos. Gock Tie and the other kids went back to work recycling their tossed waste. While the men continued to fish, the women and children collected and sent a delivery of 30,000 abalone shells to a New York button maker in 1874.

Just five years after arriving, Ah Hall and Gock Tie's tranquil fishing life was disrupted. Italian fishing boats and Portuguese whalers moved in to take over the bay. Competition for the waters became so fierce that the Portuguese rammed the Chinese sampans and cut their fishing nets. Apparently, the Chinese way of fishing, in which they would drum the sides of their sampans to drive the fish toward the nets, scared the whales away.

The Chinese resorted to filing a lawsuit against the Portuguese, but the case was dismissed. The judge ruled that the white witnesses—the Chinese themselves were not allowed to testify—were biased because of their compromising business interests with the Chinese.

To avoid further confrontation, the Point Alones Chinese switched to fishing at night. They found that by hanging pitch embers over the sides of their boats, squids would gather like moths to a flame. Ah Hall and his sons would scoop up tons of squid by the glow of lanterns and then return to shore as the Italians set out at dawn. During the day hours, Gock Tie and her mother would split and hang the squid as they learned to grow accustomed to its stench.

The smaller pieces of dried squid would be packed in salt and shipped in wooden crates back to China. The squid also provided the Chinese another resource. Gock Tie wasn't really sending squid packed in salt, but salt packed in squid. Due to British control of salt taxation in China, as much salt was smuggled into China in those days as was legally imported there.

This sneaky shipping practice provided another means of income for the Hakka. Nothing seemed to be wasted by the Point Alones Chinese, who learned to utilize every natural resource in order to have something to share with the next generation.

The Ring Game

By the turn of the twentieth century, Point Alones had grown to be the largest Chinese community in the county with 155 residents, of whom 61 were fishermen. It became even more prosperous than other Chinese settlements in cities like San Jose. Eating from patterned bamboo design porcelain bowls and drinking from four season teacups from Southern China, Gock Tie and her community enjoyed quality goods from both China and the eastern United States.

As the community grew, they developed their own distinct Chinese American culture, which combined local influences. One of Gock

Tie's childhood playmates, Quock Mui, was nicknamed Spanish Mary because she spoke five languages and translated for local Mexicans.

One event Gock Tie and Quock Mui especially looked forward to as children was the Lunar New Year festival at Point Alones. The festival drew hundreds of Chinese and non-Chinese, and the neighboring Chinese settlements in Watsonville, Santa Cruz, Salinas, and San Jose would even purchase uniforms of hometown pride and march in the opening ceremony's parade. Drawing hundreds of Chinese and non-Chinese, it culminated in the daylong Ring Game in honor of the earth god, Tu-Di Gong. The Ring Game itself, a contest in which teams of men vied for rings exploded into the air, became so intense that one participant was trampled to death by other contestants.

Gock Tie's first husband passed away in 1900, after the couple had six children. This made Gock Tie one of the few eligible Chinese women in the state of California. By this time, there was only one Chinese woman for every twenty-seven Chinese men in California. And since Chinese men couldn't marry whites, their prospects for family life were slight in the United States.

Despite the fact that she was forty-three years old, was wizened by the sea elements, and smelled like dried squid, Gock Tie must have been pretty attractive to the men around her. She probably had no shortage of suitors willing to come from as far as Marysville, the second-largest California Chinese settlement, which was 224 miles away.

My great-grandfather, Jeung Quong Chong, was the lucky winner in the ring game for Hall Gock Tie's hand in marriage. After fulfilling his labor contract in Panama, he arrived in Monterey in 1881 just before the passage of the Chinese Exclusion Act. From 1882 through 1945, this legislation barred Chinese from entry into the United States. At Point Alones, Jeung Quong Chong became such a successful businessman that the rail agent at Monterey described him as "one of the largest shippers of those days."

Not only did Quong Chong have his own fishing company and a home on the western side of Point Alones, but he also spoke Hakka like

Gock Tie. They also were roughly the same age, so they wouldn't hear of gossip about a scandalous May/December marriage. Most important, though, Gock Tie's three children still living at home lobbied on behalf of Quong Chong, according to my aunts. The children were familiar with all the single men in the village. They chimed in that they most liked Jeung Quong Chong, whom they had probably known all of their lives. In the sound wisdom of keeping household harmony, Gock Tie agreed to marry Quong Chong to placate the kids who might have been worried about getting an evil stepfather. After a simple marriage ceremony, the family moved down the street and into his home.

Perhaps because of his love of children, Jeung Quong Chong was blessed by heaven shortly thereafter. Gock Tie—at the astounding age of forty-six—bore her last child, Jeung Gwai Fong, in 1903. The family continued to fish and to work as squid driers, content within their own settlement. Gock Tie had lived at Point Alones for almost four decades by this time, and it was the only home she knew.

Her neighbors, in the meantime, grew increasingly hostile to the Chinese.

The Monterey Chinatown Fire of 1906

As the ethnic competition over fishing waters indicated, the Point Alones Chinese had uneasy relations with the local white population. Chinese even complained that when white tourists came for the Ring Game, they would feel free to enter the homes of the Chinese and steal items as souvenirs!

Anti-Chinese sentiment in the late-nineteenth century prevailed in Monterey County, as it did throughout the rest of California. In 1879, California voters considered a referendum to bar Chinese immigration. Of the 2,346 voters in Monterey County, all but one individual citizen voted for this ban.

This racism was not just limited to the political ballots, but became a program of fear and physical removal. In the neighboring Santa Cruz, huge rallies supported the Workingmen's Party and its anti-Chinese platform. Mobs bore signs that read, "America Must Never Give Up to the Chinese Invasion." Some Chinese families were purged from that town in 1885. The next year, Santa Cruz passed an ordinance banning the carrying of poles the Chinese used for laundry. It even officially sponsored a children's parade leading to an anti-Chinese rally! In 1888, Watsonville, some 26 miles north of Monterey, removed its entire Chinese community to vacant land across the Pajaro River.

By the turn of the century, the townships of Monterey and Pacific Grove had begun to encroach upon Point Alones as more American canneries were established and as the area was developed for tourism. Townspeople increased their complaints about the stench of the squid-drying operations of the Chinese.

To quell public opinion, the mayor of Monterey made a visit in 1902 to the Pacific Improvement Company, the landowners of Point Alones. On official business, he traveled to San Francisco and urged the company to end its leases to the Chinese. The Pacific Improvement Company agreed and gave notice to the Chinese that they had to vacate by February 1905.

Once again, my Hakka family was threatened with removal. This time, the enemy was not Punti peasant farmers or Portuguese whalers, but the "Big Four" of San Francisco's Nob Hill—Leland Stanford, Collis Huntington, Charles Crocker, and Mark Hopkins—and their corporate landholding company.

These robber barons exploited tens of thousands of Chinese laborers to build the Transcontinental Railroad in the 1860s. In time, the Pacific Improvement Company grew to become California's largest landowner. Even though Gock Tie's children were born and raised at Point Alones, built their own homes there before any white man owned that land, and had American citizenship by birthright, they were being forcibly evicted by the most powerful American corporation of the time.

The Chinese stalled to find an alternative site, but then the 1906 earthquake in San Francisco hit, bringing more Chinese to Point Alones seeking refuge. Gock Tie took in her two adult sons, as well as Quong Chong's brother, who had been working in San Francisco's Chinatown. Monterey's townspeople protested this influx of more Chinese and the Pacific Improvement Company feared that the community might not ever move. J. P. Pryor, the General Agent of the company, wrote to head-quarters that "the Company should undertake to use force to eject them and risk the consequences. . . . Something must be done to show the Chinese that we mean business."

What was "done" was a mysterious fire that burned down Point Alones in a mere two hours. Eight days after Pryor wrote that telegram, flames from a barn on the western end of the 100-building village quickly spread. Despite demolishing several homes to create breaks, the volunteer firemen gave up their efforts within the hour. While Gock Tie tended to her children, Quong Chong joined the other Chinese in unsuccessfully trying to protect their homes. The Chinese scrambled to retrieve what they could as white bystanders simply cheered the fire. Vandals quickly moved in to loot, and none were ever arrested.

The next morning, white residents came out to gawk at the fire's destruction, which destroyed over two-thirds of the village. A visiting German biologist took up a collection to establish a relief fund for the Chinese, but only a few donations—amounting to only $29—were collected. To finish off what the fire started, the Pacific Improvement Company built a fence around the village, and armed guards were sta-tioned to keep out the Chinese.

Gock Tie and Quong Chong, along with the rest of the Point Alones Chinese community, did not give up their land and fishing grounds easily. The fishermen tore down Pacific Improvement Company's fence and quickly put up new shacks around the western and southern edges of Point Alones. When the guards tore down the shacks, the Chinese sought legal remedies.

Not only did they sue the Pacific Improvement Company in a "Demand for Surrender of Real Property," they also charged the guards for destruction of private property. In a show of collective mobilization, thirty-five Chinese individuals, including some American-born Chinese, filed the suit. The Pacific Improvement Company offered a different location, but the Chinese had been at Point Alones for over fifty years and were loathe to move, even when confronted by America's great robber barons.

The lawsuits, however, were dismissed. After a year of struggle, the Chinese finally were pushed out of Point Alones. Gock Tie and Quong Chong initially resettled with many other Chinese on nearby McAbee Beach along Ocean View Avenue. About a quarter mile east of Point Alones, this land was within Monterey city limits, and the townspeople were repulsed by the squid-drying odors even more than before. Within a year, the city passed an ordinance forbidding the drying of squid in Monterey.

Quong Chong finally had to give up his business in 1908. By this time he was nearly blind due to diabetes, and he couldn't handle the shipping business anymore. After forty years at Point Alones, Gock Tie had lost the home her family had constructed, her family business, and the community she had helped to build.

Yet again, she and Quong Chong tasted the bitterness of being Hakka.

Now destitute, they had to move to San Francisco's Chinatown. They might not be safe from earthquakes and fire, but at least there they could be a bit insulated from the racism of looters and capitalist corporations.

It would take almost three generations before my family could climb out of the poverty and be able to live in their own homes. The Chinese village at Point Alones was eventually bulldozed into the Pacific Ocean, the only remains being small shards of porcelain bowls scattered among seashells and strands of kelp.

My mother's father didn't fare any better on Gold Mountain. He, too, had passions and the heart's desire equivalent to what Rick Warren says we should pursue to lead a purpose-driven life. Sadly, he also had only a Chinaman's chance to do so.

Undocumented Aliens
of Los Angeles

Two decades after my Hakka great-grandparents were forced from their home, my maternal grandparents moved their home within California as well. In 1926, my mother's father, Shue Hop Tin, was working as a barber in Oakland's Chinatown, but he had a bigger dream. He wanted to act in Hollywood.

His wife, Yuen Way Chon, had just given birth to their first child, Bernice, but that didn't deter him from his dream. According to his brothers who had a clothing factory in San Francisco, Hop Tin needed a larger stage that would take him from the day-to-day drudgery of the family business.

I never met my grandfather, but his dream and courage inspired me when I first heard of his aspirations. He may not have become famous or successful, but at least he followed his destiny, I believed.

You couldn't find a more unlikely person to dream of being in Hollywood movies. Shue Hop Tin came from a small farming village near Zhongshan City where the residents spoke Longdu, a dialect incomprehensible to local Cantonese. Like the Hakka, the Longdu speakers were a minority group that had to migrate to Guangdong province. They came from the adjacent Fujian Province during the Song dynasty (1023–31) and the subsequent Mongol takeover. Even though the name, Longdu, proudly translates into the "Dragon Society," the Cantonese majority saw this linguistic group as country hicks.

In the United States, the white majority saw Shue Hop Tin as an illegal alien. Shue Hop Tin was not even his real name; he had to buy a fictitious name from a Longdu neighbor in order to get through the Angel Island Immigration Station and land in San Francisco. Since the Chinese Exclusion Act of 1882 barred Chinese unless they were children of American citizens, Shue Hop Tin gave up his own identity and family name, Lowe, to start a new life in California.

Shue Hop Tin and his family were Longdu hillbillies who were out of place in both China and in California. They were right out of that old TV show, *The Beverly Hillbillies*. Even the show's theme song, "The Ballad of Jed Clampett," described them to a tee: "Poor mountaineer, barely kept his family fed. . . . They loaded up the truck and moved to Beverly (Hills, that is, swimming pools, movie stars)."[5]

The only thing different was that the Los Angeles neighborhood where Shue Hop Tin moved had no swimming pools. The Old Chinatown in Los Angeles, founded by laundrymen, vegetable peddlers, and agricultural and railroad workers in the 1800s, had been in slow decline after the Chinese Exclusion Act. Although their numbers grew in Los Angeles, the Chinese never were able to purchase property or even rise above subsistence incomes.

Since railroad tracks ran right through Chinatown, developers after the turn of the century planned to raze it and construct Union Station there. These owners had so little regard for their lessees that they didn't bother to pave the streets. The Chinese languished in abject living conditions as the redevelopment of downtown Los Angeles bogged down. Twenty years passed before the California Supreme Court finally approved the condemnation of Old Chinatown and the construction of the new Union Station in 1931.

One proposal for the poor Chinese at that time was to relocate them and use them as tourist attractions. The result was China City. Replete with Hollywood movie sets, China City in the '30s was an exoticized vision of what Americans expected of the Orient. Tourists could even take rickshaw rides around the winding Chinese alleys to watch acrobats perform and traditional artists carve jewelry. Two major fires, however, prevented the place from making profits, and it eventually closed by 1950.

Other Chinese Americans moved to the racially mixed South Central Los Angeles neighborhood of East Adams. Allowed there because it was poor and already full of people of color, the Chinese community soon grew large enough to host the Chinese Presbyterian Church and a Chinese school. Shue Hop Tin and Yuen Way Chon relocated to a duplex in this neighborhood, where they had three more children: Gilbert, Georgia, and Sidney. For part of their income, Hop Tin used his truck to go to the piers and pick up fresh fish, which he resold to neighbors.

These neighbors included African American families who made up the majority of the community. The Shues were so close to the next-door neighbors in their duplex that they even split the use of a phone. Whenever Shue Hop Tin or my mother, Bernice, got a telephone call, their neighbors would simply call them over and pass the phone at the porch. The kids bored a half-dollar-sized hole through the wall so they could talk at night. Bernice even has a Southern black drawl to this day, pronouncing doll as "dawl." "You folks look at that cutie Barbie dawl!" my mom would exclaim, and I would look for a long, pointed spike.

Hollywood Dreams

Shue Hop Tin and Bernice needed that phone because sometimes, their Hollywood casting agent would call them. In my fantasies to be special, I grandiosely imagined I was the grandson of Fu Manchu. Or, at least, I was the grandson of the actor who played Fu Manchu, which made me kind of cool by association.

In the '30s, if a Chinese American male like Shue Hop Tin ever were to get a role, it would be to play Fu Manchu. Opposite the all-American hero, Fu Manchu was a diabolical mastermind hell-bent on world domination. Not only was he nefarious, but he was a genius who obtained four doctorates in Western universities and could use both Western and Eastern technologies for evil. Failing to overthrow the Chinese government in the Boxer Rebellion, Fu Manchu and his family turned their intentions to the global drug trade and white slavery. Even the sight of him—with sly eyes and long whiskers dripping off the sides of his mouth—was devilish.

We have only two photographs of my grandfather. One is a wedding shot in which Shue Hop Tin, in a Western suit, stands next to my seated grandmother. The other is a black-and-white Hollywood publicity still. I saw it briefly one time when I was rummaging through an old box of photos, and it became the basis for my Fu Manchu fancies. Draped in a long silk gown with a dragon-design, Shue Hop Tin stands impassively in front of Chinese screens that hide the mysteries of the Orient. A Tang Dynasty mandarin hat sits atop his long locks, which add to his towering menace. Snow-white whiskers flow to his chest. At his side, a few young white women fawn over him.

When I pictured my grandfather, I saw Fu Manchu. Arch villains always were more interesting characters to me than the good guys, because their sinister plots involved warped thinking and elaborate scheming. With complicated backgrounds, they usually held mixed motives gone awry. Along with conniving and machinating as I did, TV and movie villains often looked like me, which was a plus.

Years later when I rediscovered the publicity still, I was surprised to see that my grandfather didn't appear as evil as I had imagined. Instead, he was placidly reading a book, more like the Chinese god of literature. It turned out that my memory was constructed by an American stereotype, my fantasy fueled by Hollywood depictions.

This real photo displayed how the West viewed the East. My grandfather appeared traditional and stoic; the young white girls in bathing suits next to him were youthful and free-spirited. In fact, it also revealed how the West saw itself: as modern and progressive, unlike the exotic and strange Orientals.

The flip side of the villainous Hollywood Oriental was that of the peasant, noble but victimized. The 1937 film, *The Good Earth*, recounted the saga of a poor peasant, Wang Lung, who married a homely, former slave girl, O-Lan. Both were tragic characters, who suffered even when falling upon good fortune. Set against the backdrop of drought, famine, and civil chaos, the Chinese peasants were often seen solely as mobs that loot homes or flee locusts. In the films during this period, white actors in yellowface played the lead roles as Chinese.

If my grandfather looked like the incarnation of evil, my mother and uncle were pictures of innocence and helplessness when they worked as Hollywood extras. My mother, Bernice, and her brother, Gilbert, acted their parts as grubby, penniless waifs, which wasn't difficult because that's who they actually were. When not singing giddily as charming little natives of Shangri-la in *Lost Horizon*, they were screaming, peasant folk fleeing locusts in *The Good Earth*. To this day, my mom's body of Hollywood work consists of her screaming incomprehensibly. In another movie she made in her seventies, her part involved shrieking at the sight of a Chinatown murder.

Bernice also had a part in a movie that, as she recalls, had Shanghai in the title. We can't find the exact film, however, because dozens of Hollywood films featured Shanghai in the '30s and '40s. Conjuring up excitement, mystery, and danger, the very name of Shanghai meant to be kidnapped. Hollywood looked at Shanghai from all sides. Films included *East of Shanghai* (1931), *West of Shanghai* (1937), and *North of Shanghai* (1939). Residents living south of Shanghai should be miffed that their perspective was omitted.

Whether the villain or the victim, the Oriental in Hollywood films was exotic, foreign, and inscrutable. The ways the West saw the East shaped how I saw my family and, by extension, myself. The Chinese side of me is weird and old-fashioned; my American side is normal.

I wonder if Shue Hop Tin was bemused by getting paid for such frivolous work or disgusted and ashamed by colluding in the negative depiction of his race. In all probability, he must have felt a mixture of both. I realize now that his Hollywood dream wasn't to make art or to gain fame; it was just to get the easiest work available to Chinese, even if it came only sporadically.

Sadly, the only way to break the stereotype of Chinese as cheap labor and to earn more was to act in movies as a stereotype. Chinese Americans weren't seen as individuals or treated as such, but only as foreign villains and helpless hordes.

Separation Anxiety

Despite looking like a strong, ageless criminal, my grandfather died at the relatively young age of forty-seven from complications due to tuberculosis. The fact that he was Chinese contributed to his illness.

Chinese Americans got this disease not because they were genetically predisposed to it, but because of the housing policies that kept them confined to tight, communal quarters, where they could more easily spread the infection. My grandmother, Yuen Way Chon, was also diagnosed with the illness in 1942, and she was sent to Olive View Hospital. With no antibiotic for tuberculosis discovered yet, she had to lie on her back, with a sandbag on her chest, for hours on end.

With their father gone and their mother in quarantine, the Shue children had no legal guardian in their home. They continued to act in order to avoid being split apart.

But instead of working as extras in movies, they acted as an intact family and they pretended to live with a guardian. In this way, they could stay together and receive county welfare checks. In actuality, they lived secretly on their own.

When I heard that my mom and her siblings were left to their own devices, I pictured her eating candy for dinner, my uncles never washing, and the house a mess. What happened was that Bernice, only fifteen years old herself, took care of her siblings as they paid rent, shopped for groceries, and attended school by themselves. Only when the social worker came did an adult neighbor show up to play her role as fictive kin.

Bernice remembers that time period matter-of-factly: "I just kept everybody together. The kids were good so we had no problem. I felt pretty secure because we had some relatives down the street." After almost a year of living on the sly while their mom remained at the sanitorium, their secret life unraveled. Bernice was diagnosed with tuberculosis at school, so the county made a surprise home inspection of their apartment.

"The day the social worker came was the worst day of my life," Gilbert said bitterly, recalling the day the social worker made a home visit and found no adult. Recognizing that the Shue children were living unattended, the social workers did in fact traumatize the children and split them apart from each other. Bernice was sent to Olive View Hospital, and the other three—ages fourteen, twelve, and ten—were sent to boarding schools in the county.

While Bernice and her siblings were not black, they certainly were not white and could not be sent to white foster homes in Los Angeles. As early as 1923, the San Francisco Bay Area had a few Chinese orphanages, such as the Chung Mei Home for boys in Berkeley and El Cerrito and the Ming Quong Home for girls in Oakland and Los Gatos. Los Angeles, on the other hand, had no such facilities. The county assigned the Shue children to the only place where Chinese kids in a black neighborhood could go in segregated Los Angeles: a boarding school for Mexican Americans.

Gilbert and Sydney were sent to the Spanish American Institute (SAI), a sprawling "ranchito" of thirty acres in Gardena, California. Founded in 1931 by the Methodist Episcopal Church and its Latin American Conference, its aims were threefold: to instill within the boys Christian character; to produce men with vocational skills; and to develop a group of "race leaders" who would return to Mexico or the Mexican American community to minister.

Georgia was sent alone to the SAI's sister school, the Frances DePauw School for Girls on Sunset Boulevard in Los Angeles. In the 1940s, the school hosted almost two hundred girls who also were trained to become race leaders, which meant becoming suitable Latina wives for the boys of SAI and Christian mothers.

The Shue siblings spent the remainder of their youth at these Mexican boarding homes and picked up Spanish as their home language. They became model students, with Gilbert being elected as the school's town mayor and later attending Cal Poly San Luis Obispo. Sidney became an All-American football player at Pepperdine University, and Georgia eventually joined her sister to go to City College of San Francisco.

SAI proved quite effective in developing Chinese race leaders for the Mexican community. Upon graduation, Gilbert returned to teach at SAI and served as a residential director. He later became a successful dairy farmer and then founded another business—an enterprising worm farm—which was able to employ many local Mexican Americans.

On his eightieth birthday, Gilbert's family feted him with a traditional Chinese banquet: shark fin soup, abalone with vegetables, Peking duck, and longevity noodles. In a large dining hall surrounded by family and friends, Gilbert gave a prepared, bilingual thank you speech. First, he thanked his family in English. Next he expressed his appreciation to his friends—not in Chinese, but in Spanish! So many SAI alumni attended, that ending the evening with a carousing Mexican birthday song, "Las Mananitas," for this Chinese son of Fu Manchu seemed strangely appropriate.

In spite of the roles fixed in place for Orientals, my mom's family ended up far from traditional. Through the vagaries of segregation and racism, California produced an illegal alien Hollywood actor, a teenage welfare mom with a black Southern drawl, a Spanish-speaking worm farmer from a Mexican school, and an All-American football player, all from within the same Chinese family.

Chinatown, USA

Just as being Chinese led to my great-grandmother's displacement, my grandfather's assumed identity, and my mother's broken childhood, being Chinese shaped my father's fortunes and subsequently, mine.

As my mother Bernice grew up in ghettoized South Central Los Angeles, my father Albert lived in San Francisco's Chinatown, where de facto segregation kept Chinese in that celebrated ethnic enclave. By the '40s, Chinatown had transformed its image from a plague-filled, labyrinthian zone of underground opium dens and brothels into a fun, kitschy tourist attraction of the Far East. At the same time, the residents like my aunts and uncles grew up with a uniquely Chinese American flavor.

Because Chinese Americans had to take care of themselves, Chinatown was institutionally complete. Businesses, organizations, and agencies served the community from cradle to grave. My uncles could be born at the Chinese Hospital, attend American public school at the "Oriental School," and get married at First Chinese Baptist Church. They would celebrate a Chinese New Year banquet with the On Ping Family Association and then go eat apple pie at Sun Wah Kue for a late-night snack. When it was time to go, Chinese Americans would march out after a Taoist funeral service at Green Street Mortuary.

The Chinese of San Francisco also developed parallel institutions to meet all sorts of needs and services that they were excluded from outside Chinatown. Since the *San Francisco Chronicle* did not cover Chinese American issues, the *Chung Sai Yat Po* newspaper published daily editorials. The Pacific Bell Telephone and Telegraph Company did not service Chinatown, so the Chinese Telephone Exchange opened, where the operators had to remember nearly 1,500 names and speak multiple Chinese dialects. When they wanted a night out swing dancing, my dad and his friends had their pick of twelve night clubs, such as the Kubla Khan, the Shangri-La, and Forbidden City.

Each of these parallel institutions was distinctly American. Albert belonged to one of the many sports clubs in Chinatown, the Flying Eagles, which participated in tournaments of baseball, football, and basketball. They also played a form of street volleyball with nine to a team. In 1900, Chinese rallied to support their town in the Lunar New Year Ring Game; by 1950, sold-out crowds of 4,000 Chinese Americans cheered at Golden Gate Park's Kezar Pavilion to root for their favorite basketball club. Given his tall height for a Chinese American—5 feet 10 inches—Albert got picked to join an all-star San Francisco Chinese team, the Saints. My father kept a news clipping of their 1947 West Coast tour, in which they won a national, Pan-Asian American tournament against Japanese from Chicago and Filipinos from Hawaii.

Albert remembered Chinatown fondly, as a place "where everyone knew everyone else," and young people stayed up and went out for *siu yeh*, late-night snacks. If they didn't want to eat out, they could order, get meals delivered, and then simply leave the dishes outside their front door. Chinatown restaurants had room service for the entire neighborhood.

Despite the romanticized narratives of Albert's childhood, the establishment of parallel institutions, and the comfort of knowing everyone, Chinatown was still a place on the margins, which constantly reminded its residents of their impoverished status and their stigmatized race. The stark reality was that Chinatown was ghettoized and Chinese had to stay in their place. Opportunities for the adults remained limited in the '40s, such that Chinese American men remained relegated to houseboy, laundryman, or restaurant worker. The housing conditions weren't great either. The densest neighborhood in the United States outside of Manhattan, San Francisco Chinatown's residences were substandard and pest-ridden. Families often lived in hotels built for single men and occupied 8-by-10-foot rooms that had shared bathrooms and kitchens. Albert, like many of his peers, rationally chose to move out as soon as he could.

Affirmative Action
for Whites and Chinese

Every now and then I caught flashes of my family's financial hardships and the bitter side of living in Chinatown. If you searched his dresser drawers, you would find that Albert kept dollars stuffed in socks and pockets. Having to scrounge for work since the age of five, he needed to have some pocket money around all the time for security.

It took armed strife and war to change the Jeung family's opportunities in California.

Jeung Gwai Fong, Hall Gock Tie's son and my grandfather, dropped out of the Oriental School in the fifth grade when he had to go to work. Chinese may value education, but if a degree couldn't land a Chinese person in the U.S. a job, why bother? Jeung Gwai Fong turned to peeling shrimp and cutting potatoes on San Francisco's waterfront to help his blind parents survive.

Then one day, as the old saying goes, Jeung Gwai Fong got "hit in the head with a brick," and his luck turned around. Since he worked on the waterfront and was a burly, able-bodied man, Jeung Gwai Fong got enlisted into the 1934 West Coast Waterfront Strike to shut down the port. The four-day strike turned violent as police shot tear gas into the crowds and killed two men on Bloody Thursday. The mayor called a state of emergency, and the National Guard, armed with machine guns, moved in to quell the strike.

For his sacrifice of a lifetime of headaches from the brick injury, Jeung Gwai Fong was able to obtain a job at a union shop mixing hair care products. He was so grateful to get a decent wage for once that he named his youngest daughter Alva, after a hair gel!

While Jeung Gwai Fong became a union laborer, his wife, Ho Lin Chun, was busy being pregnant and raising nine children. Fortunately for her, World War II interrupted her stay-at-home mothering duties. With many men at war and African Americans winning concessions from the president to end discriminatory hiring, opportunities finally opened up for women and for Chinese.

Instead of sitting around eating watermelon seeds and chatting with her friends at the Chinese opera theater up the street, Ho Lin Chun was able to get her first job because of the war effort. In joining the likes of Rosie the Riveter, Lin Chun the Floor Sweeper got paid to sit around, eat watermelon seeds, and chat with her friends at Hunter's Point Naval Shipyard. What made the job even sweeter was that she didn't have her pesky children around her all the time.

The war against fascism brought freedom to many fronts. Along with the federal government, the U.S. Postal Service also began hiring a high number of Chinese in San Francisco. My Uncle Tom was one of these beneficiaries and ended up working as a mail carrier for thirty-five years.

Albert was the family's biggest beneficiary of wartime affirmative action. After serving in the military, he took advantage of the G.I. Bill for a college grant and a housing loan. He attended San Francisco State University, majored in accounting, and met his future wife, Bernice, there. Together they purchased a home in San Francisco's Richmond District as one of its first Chinese families. Chinese Americans who bought in the Richmond District eventually struck it rich, since housing prices in San Francisco skyrocketed in the '80s.

With his professional degree and home ownership, Albert was able to ascend to the ranks of the upper middle class and send his children to good schools. He financed our college tuitions by purchasing even more real estate with the equity of his first home. My siblings and I were thus able to afford to go to graduate schools and become professionals as well.

Albert's younger siblings didn't all take advantage of the G.I. Bill. Either they could not, because they were female and never enlisted, or they simply chose not to attend college. Without the assistance of the G.I. Bill, these siblings had a much tougher time financially. They stayed in working class jobs, such as postal work, furniture sales, and hairstyling. My cousins, subsequently, went to schools with fewer resources than where my sibling and I attended. They now work as chefs, clerks, and car alarm salespeople. Within our generation, the income gap between cousins is stark.

My father and his siblings had the same parents, genetic makeup, cultural upbringing, and environmental influences. One received help from the G.I. Bill and rose from poverty to become a millionaire in one generation. The others, pulling themselves up by their bootstraps, also did well but certainly aren't as wealthy. The clear difference is that one—my father—received the federal government's assistance.

Multiply what happened within my family a million times over and you can see why today's American racial wealth gap is so severe. African American veterans could not take advantage of the G.I. Bill, but whites were able to move to middle-class suburbs. African Americans had to be more self-reliant, but were trapped in poor neighborhoods with few job opportunities. By 1984, the year that many G.I. Bill mortgages matured and I graduated from college, the net worth of whites was ten times that of African Americans.

My siblings and I *seem* to have turned out as Chinese American successes. We have our own homes and have raised cute kids, who have all been accepted into University of California campuses. These universities are perfect for Chinese, since they're prestigious as well as inexpensive (relatively!). This model minority status, however, wasn't based solely on our hard work and intelligence. We benefited from a policy that was enacted two decades before I was born.

Just as racialized policies affected Chinese American housing and family life for my grandparents, they also influenced Chinese American prospects and success for my parents and myself.

Equal Treatment of Inequality

It turns out that my family's stories aren't unique or special. In fact, my forebears suffered from the same onerous policies and disparate treatment that other Chinese in the United States received. My great-grandmother was forcibly removed from her home in Point Alones—purged just like the 300 other Chinese communities that were driven out throughout the West Coast in the nineteenth century. Officially excluded from this country, my grandfather gave up his name and became a paper son. So many Chinese, likewise, claimed to be American citizens that every Chinese woman in the United States before 1906 would have had to have given birth to 600 babies! My mother, stricken by tuberculosis, was quarantined and watched as her siblings were separated into different foster homes. My father's siblings were taken from their parents for the same reason. After catching this disease by living in crowded, squalid conditions, Chinese were three times more likely to die from tuberculosis than whites in San Francisco.

Treated disparately as a group, we Chinese Americans suffered similar racial consequences—purged, segregated, stereotyped, impoverished, and struck ill. In resistance, the Chinese fought back together. My ancestors defended their livelihoods and homes. They filed lawsuits and directly tore down the fences that were keeping them out. Bypassing unjust laws, they assumed different identities and maintained their own secret residences. They established their own culture of Ring Games and basketball tournaments, of Chinese schools and midnight snacking.

When Chinese did get ahead in the United States, it was because we were beneficiaries of collective efforts. Longshoremen fought for the union rights that got my grandfather a decent wage. African Americans seeking integration opened up jobs for my grandmother and uncles. Veterans defending our country obtained special entitlements that boosted my father out of poverty.

I am not that unique, but an object of racial Orientalism like other Chinese. I am not very special, just an heir to class privilege that made me who I am. Rather than trying to see myself as a self-made individual and star of my own Disney movie, I have come to recognize the impacts of race and class.

American Success Story

I am tempted to claim my family as an ethnic American success story. Whereas my great-grandmother and great-grandfather got evicted by Governor Leland Stanford Jr., I later got to attend Stanford University. Through my networks from Stanford, I was able to obtain a job with Mayor Art Agnos of San Francisco. And with the credentials of my university degree, I entered a doctoral program at UC Berkeley and eventually taught ethnic studies and the legacy of my people.

It seems like what man intended for harm, God intended for good. My entrance into the ranks of the American privileged may be understood as God's redemptive and merciful action.

In fact, I don't have to be Hakka anymore, but can claim to be Chinese, just as many Hakka have shed their tribal ancestry. I can take pride in Hakka leaders such as Sun Yat-sen, the founding father of modern China; Deng Xiaoping, the leader of the Chinese Community Party who steered its economic liberalization; or Lee Kuan Yew, the first prime minister of Singapore. They were so successful that they became Chinese leaders, and their Hakka background did not hold them back. In fact, they easily shed their Hakka identities, didn't refer to their heritage, and instead operated as simply Han Chinese. Like them, I could pass for Chinese and claim five thousand years of glorious history and tradition.

Or why even bother choosing Chinese ancestors as my role models? As a fifth-generation Californian, I could just as well choose to be part of America, God's "chosen nation," and claim its privileges in post-racial America. I certainly have been a beneficiary of its entitlements and wealth.

Just as Pastor Warren recommends, I could look at my gifts and abilities to see how I am uniquely fit to serve God's kingdom. God redeems all history, even my family's Hakka and Chinese racialized experiences, and wants us to pursue our heart's desire.

However, this task of self-exploration of one's call—necessary to become effective and successful, according to Reverend Warren—contributes to my identity angst. I have to figure out my abilities. I need to discern what I authentically desire. I have to get an actual personality, so that I can express myself. And I need a range of experiences that God will use to prepare me.

Assimilating into post-racial American society and seeing myself simply as someone who can't be categorized would be freeing. I could just be myself and be whomever I want to be. Identifying as God's beloved child is also redemptive. It would help me feel special and at peace with who I am.

Unfortunately, my problem with developing a healthy self-esteem and discovering my identity is that I get too self-absorbed while singing and looking at myself in the mirror. Even though I know this narcissistic orientation helps the economy through the purchase of skin and hair products to make me feel good about myself, this ironically patriotic selflessness doesn't help me get over myself.

Another, more complicated issue with American individualism and identity is that not all people have the opportunity to reach their full potential. For many of us, if not most, how we look and how we're treated—as members of a group and not just as individuals—are a racial uniform that straitjackets us. My family's experiences as Chinese in the United States are typical in this regard.

Ancestral Choices

I am Hakka, a guest person. My identity derives from a simple, agrarian people who lived on the hillsides that no one wanted, dressed in black, and wore hats with curtains. And ate food that looked like crap.

My family in the United States were working class, people of color. They were victims of institutional discrimination, forcible removal, segregation, stereotyping, and underemployment.

I am grateful that God redeems this history. Yet, along with this redemption, I am reclaiming this history and my identity as Chinese Hakka.

In looking to our pasts, Ralph Ellison wrote, "Some people are your relatives but others are your ancestors, and you choose the ones you want to have as ancestors. You create yourself out of those values."[6]

I am choosing the Hakka as my ancestors, attempting to create myself from their values. That's how I can draw closer to Jesus, his compassion, and his ways. It's not the only identity I embrace nor is it necessarily the best one to become like Jesus. Living as a guest, nonetheless, provides helpful alternatives to American individualistic thinking.

Jesus himself was like a Hakka. Biblical history recounts a narrative of a loose confederation of people, the Hebrews, who were lowly desert nomads, exiled refugees, and colonized minorities. Traveling from Judah to Egypt as persecuted refugees, Jesus' family had no choice about where they would live.

Jesus did not reside in his ancestral city, Bethlehem, and he had no homeland, much like the Hakka. His family lived in Galilee, a region known for political autonomy and violent resistance. Residents from Nazareth, his backwater village in the hills were sometimes mocked as evil, as evidenced by Nathanael's question, "Can anything good come from Nazareth?" (John 1:46).

Once Jesus began his ministry, he was a guest person. The Messiah wandered as a migrant worker from town to town with no place to rest his head. He did not have citizenship in Rome, although he had to pay taxes to the empire. To those who encountered him, "He was despised and rejected by mankind, a man of suffering, and familiar with pain" (Isaiah 53:3).

Jesus lived the life of the Hakka. If I am to understand him, I need to be a guest person myself.

Further, if I am to follow in his footsteps and ministry, I should find solidarity with the Hakka and others similarly marginalized. Such a solidarity enables us to act justly, to love mercy, and to walk humbly. Jesus identified with the poor and suffering and was moved with compassion for them. He didn't love them from afar, but left the riches of heaven in order to sympathize with human weaknesses and travails here on earth.

Surprisingly, Jesus wants fellowship with sinners such as I. Calling them his friends, he joined with traitorous tax collectors, shameful prostitutes, and unclean lepers throughout his ministry. He died so that we can be reconciled to God and to each other across racial and class lines. I, too, want the joy of that kind of fellowship. Solidarity with the Hakka and the poor gift me with the close belonging, joint purpose, and communal peace that God intended for his people.

Finally, learning the ways of the Hakka shows how to live lightly here on earth. The Hebrews in Babylon also faced the temptation to conform to the land of their exile. To protect them, God sent prophets who warned them to remember who they were and where they came from. They were to be simply guests in that empire, separate in their ways and beliefs. Similarly, we need to be holy through our simplicity and generosity, just as Daniel sought to be undefiled by Nebuchadnezzar's power and riches. We should be set apart by our solidarity with the poor and concern for the common good, just as Nehemiah aimed to do as he rebuilt Jerusalem's walls.

Later, Paul and Peter wrote to remind the Christians in the Roman empire of their resident alien status. Paul wrote to the Philippians how he counted every earthly accomplishment a loss, especially in light of his citizenship in heaven. Peter, too, instructed the diasporic church in the provinces of Asia Minor to live out their status as foreigners and exiles to this world. To lead holy lives, he reminded us, is to see ourselves as "a chosen people, a royal priesthood, a holy nation, God's special possession" (1 Peter 2:9–10).

I may not be special, but I am blessed to be part of God's special possession. As I reclaim my Hakka roots and learn the values of being a guest, then perhaps I can know how to journey like Jesus.

CHAPTER 3

Guests and Hosts
of People of Peace

One autumn afternoon, Carl, an African American high school sophomore, walked down East 16th Street in the Murder Dubs to return to Oak Park from school. Two dope runners about his age, who had been harassing him about carrying a backpack, yelled at him even more aggressively that day. Maybe they were drunk, maybe they were bored and needed some action. Small for his age and baby-faced, Carl ignored them as he walked quickly toward the complex's parking lot.

The two young men straightened from their crouches against the fence post and blocked Carl's path. Tensing, he slowed so he could maneuver around them.

"Carl!" boomed an adult voice from inside the parking lot. "Come over here! I want to talk to you." Kosal, normally soft-spoken, met Carl halfway and asked him about his day as they walked to the courtyard. The runners glared at their backs, but returned to leaning without making further comments.

Once inside the courtyard, Kosal abruptly quit the conversation and went upstairs. Carl was confused about their chat and wondered, "Uh, what am I supposed to do now?" Shrugging his shoulders and shaking his head in bewilderment, he entered his own apartment.

Only later did Carl realize that Kosal was speaking to him solely to protect him from the other boys.

Jesus' Command to Be Guests

After moving from Oakland and living in Las Vegas and Spokane for over ten years, Carl returned in 2009 to visit Oak Park, which by then had been remodeled. While the complex looked completely different, he did recognize some Cambodian men who were playing a Khmer form of Hacky Sack, just as they had when he was a kid. They hugged him and said, "Your dad is over there."

"My dad?" wondered Carl. Then he caught sight of Kosal. Others knew what Carl had felt. "I have a mom and a dad," he confided to me, "but Kosal was there for me when I needed him the most. I have this family that saved me from going a different path."

Although Kosal and his family were refugees, exiled from Cambodia to a new land, they were hosts to Carl and me at Oak Park. From them, we received hospitality and protection from the neighborhood's hostile environment. According to Asian norms of hospitality, hosts don't ask guests what they want, but instead assume what they want and meet those needs. They recognize that travelers are tired, so they tell guests to sit. They are aware that those on the road must be thirsty, so they automatically give visitors something to drink. They recognize that those new to a town need help in a dangerous setting, so they risk their own safety for their guests as Kosal did for Carl. The guest's role is to receive gladly both the succor and relationship based on mutual aid.

Just as the Hakka are guest families, often at the mercy of those already living on the land, followers of Jesus also are sent out as guests. We are to look for "people of peace," those like Kosal and my other neighbors at Oak Park, to host us. In Luke, Jesus commanded his followers: "Go! I am sending you out like lambs among wolves. Do not take a purse or bag or sandals; and do not greet anyone on the road. When you enter a house, first say, 'Peace to this house.' If someone who promotes peace is there, your peace will rest on them; if not, it will return to you. Stay there, eating and drinking whatever they give you" (Luke 10:3–7).

Instead of ministering with well-dressed strategies or impressive displays of wealth, Jesus taught his followers to be like lambs, meek and vulnerable. Rather than being self-sufficient and independent, followers of Christ are to go in twos, live simply, and rely on those with whom we share the good news. Trusting in the message that the kingdom of God is near, we do not have to concern ourselves about how we appear or what we have. In contrast, we are to accept whatever can be offered by our hosts, no matter who they are, and not seek better accommodations.

At Oak Park, we Christians who relocated there encountered numerous people of peace who welcomed us. Some were gangsters, a few were considered "illegal," and one didn't even have a home. Nonetheless, they invited us into their lives. As we sought to reciprocate their gracious hospitality with our resources and gifts, we found joy in our love and service to one another. Who would know that twenty years later we could still see the power of Jesus at work in their lives and our own?

Urban Ministry as Guests and Hosts

Doing ministry as guests to people of peace subverts the normal power dynamics of Western missionary and evangelistic efforts. In the past, Protestant Christianity and American missionaries arrived in China with force. China had to fight the Opium Wars with Britain and other colonizing nations in the mid-nineteenth century to prevent the trade of the drug within its borders. Anglo-French forces defeated the Chinese, forcing them to open their ports, legalize opium trade, and allow missionaries to travel throughout the country. The signing of the Treaty of Nanking in 1842 represented the start of China's "century of humiliation." Not surprisingly, Christianity was viewed in China as a foreign religion and missionaries' efforts were largely rebuffed.

Likewise, the Spanish entered California and established not only missions, but also presidios and pueblos in the 1700s and 1800s. The introduction of Christianity with political conquest and economic super-exploitation through slavery resulted in the unfortunate conflation of religion with "guns, germs, and steel." The germs brought by the Spanish tragically wiped out at least 75 percent of California's indigenous population through disease. These cases are not isolated; sadly, the history of Christian missions throughout the world is replete with stories of cultural and human genocide through Western colonization.

Today, Christians continue to wrestle with how to use their earthly privilege and power in order to minister, serve, and invite others to follow Jesus' ways. According to Andy Crouch, one strategy is for Christians—especially the elite in art, media, and technology—to use their skills of culture-making for the flourishing of cities.[1] Due to globalization and urbanization, revitalization of metropolitan areas is crucial to the transformation of broader society. Since cultural changes flow from urban centers such as New York and Los Angeles, Christians are to seek the redemption of these cities and others.

This effort of Christians to cultivate the values, norms, and ideals of our society is part of our "cultural mandate" to be creative, as God was creative. Tim Keller, megachurch pastor of Redeemer Presbyterian Church, justifies this strategy: "Through the cities, Christians changed history and culture by winning the elites as well as identifying deeply with the poor."[2]

I appreciate Crouch's and Keller's balanced approach of working with both elites and the poor, for Jesus spoke to both kings and lepers. Yet I question how urban churches can do both well. While elites have the financial capital, political power, and cultural resources to develop and enrich cities, they often do so through the exploitation and marginalization of the poor. As much as urban Christians might develop a neighborhood, they also gentrify and displace the poor. Christian elites—like myself—employing Keller's model often find ourselves in the contradictory position of wanting to identify deeply with the poor, but complicit in a system of economic and cultural domination.

Christians may want to support the flourishing of cities, yet they cannot escape the logic of capitalism that exploits people throughout the world as disposable labor markets. Our economy, furthermore, degrades the environment as we manufacture, sell, purchase, and throw away more and more stuff. It also holds a cultural monopoly, in which almost every conceivable space becomes an advertisement, aimed at increasing profits. We are thus enmeshed in an economic and cultural system of exploitation; how can we dare imagine to re-create it?

Another issue I have is that these authors assume that Christian culture-makers have the power to produce and disseminate their ideas, writings, and art. Keller thus recommends that as resident aliens, Christians in the city are "to be fully involved in its life, working in it and praying for it."[3] However, as seen in the stories of my family, people of color often are not even included in the cultural or civic life of mainstream America. Crouch's and Keller's assumptions are that (1) Christians have the power to shape broader culture without compromising themselves; and that (2) each Christian shares equally in this power. These presumptions may be true for the audiences whom they seek to reach. However, I believe they write to only a small percentage of individuals who have the capacity and audacity to seek societal transformation.

Ministry as Hakka—being sent out to be guests—may offer an approach that establishes a different relationship between the minister and the ministered, between the creative class and the urban poor. It acknowledges that God is already moving among people of peace, and that disciples humbly enter into the work that God has already started. Our role as guests is not to remake our host community, but simply to receive and reciprocate peace.

We minister with the attitude of grateful guests, but we also must recognize our calling to be gracious hosts. After years of living at Oak Park, we Christians had been around long enough to host neighbors in our apartments and to share our resources with them. From these families, we learned practices of hospitality that were valued in biblical times and exemplified in the Good Samaritan parable. We then sought to do the same: to be available and present to meet our guests' needs; to offer help and healing; and to protect and advocate for their interests.

Ministering as grateful guests and as gracious hosts acknowledges the different levels of power, privilege, and resources we had at Oak Park. Peace, though, was something we all could promote and share.

Sent to Live Simply

For the decade that Dan and I lived at Oak Park, we slept like monks. Or at least, how I imagine monks sleep. Dan constructed a wooden table that folded out from the wall, and he went to bed on top of that platform, with a blanket as padding. I slept on the floor on a bamboo beach mat that cost one dollar in Chinatown. The woven mat would fray over time, so I would have to buy myself a new bed about once a year. I didn't have to make my bed in the morning so much as I had to squash my down sleeping bag into its stuff sack and roll up my mat. In the winters, I slept in this sleeping bag within another sleeping bag because our heating didn't work well. We were warm enough and didn't have back problems, so I assume monks sleep equally well.

Our 450-square-foot apartment was as austere as a monastery cell, too. We ripped out the carpet because of its cat smell, so our flooring was made of mustard brown, asbestos tiles. For furnishing, we placed the backseat of my minivan in the living room; most sofas don't have moveable armrests like we had. We had no stereo system, DVD player, or even a television for most of the time. I was scared of being warped by advertising like I had been in Hong Kong, so I avoided TV and its commercials. If I wanted to watch sports, I went upstairs and enjoyed the company of my neighbors, who had cable television.

We certainly didn't personalize our apartment with any artwork. Since we held English as a Second Language classes and a tutoring program in our home, we put up alphabet wallpaper borders. With a whiteboard on our bookshelf, our apartment was an after-school classroom half the week.

When guests came, we would scramble to get chairs for everyone. Our neighbors didn't have many, as the Cambodians ate on mats on their floors. Part of our bachelor charm at Oak Park—or so we thought—was that visitors had to dine while seated on 5-gallon plastic bins turned upside down. Oftentimes, our meal conversations were made difficult by the ruckus of children playing outside. It was like going to see the musical *Stomp* and then eating while sitting on the drums.

Having grown up with the *Brady Bunch* in the '70s as I had, Dan was raised in a large family in the suburb of Burlingame. Both his grandfather and great-grandfather were doctors, and he planned to pursue a health career as well. But then he had a charismatic, born-again experience in high school and spent nine months with the missions group Youth With A Mission in the Philippines.

That mission was harrowing yet exhilarating for Dan. The village where he stayed was bombed by government forces, who believed insurgents were hiding in nearby hills. The villagers merely wanted to farm the land, but the government sought to appropriate their property. Dan couldn't fathom the government's policy. "Seeing the fighting firsthand challenged my initial assumption that governments can't be that bad. But they are," shuddered Dan. "It was completely awful, and I was in there with them."

Dan also realized that his own suburban lifestyle and upbringing had been based on the exploitation of the poor; the workers who grew his food and made his clothes were just like his friends in the Philippines who grew crops to be exported but couldn't afford to eat their own harvest. He realized, "I had all my views challenged. My comfortable, suburban experience came at the expense of other people and what they're going through. Being connected in the Philippines with those people—experiencing that oppression—made me want to live differently."

He returned from this mission trip living differently from his suburban upbringing and choosing to dwell among the urban poor. Staff at Harbor House, a Christian nonprofit neighborhood center in Oakland's San Antonio district, jokingly recommended that he move into Oak

Park Apartments, which was as close to a developing country as possible in the United States. To their surprise, he did.

Wanting to support his neighbors, Dan began a housecleaning business that was doing moderately well when I met him. Although he had a white, Catholic upbringing and I had a Chinese, fundamentalist background, we shared some eerie similarities that made living together at Oak Park easy for us. We were born in the same year, and our fathers, who grew up during the Depression, taught us how to be stingy and live simply. We could survive like roaches, eating deprived diets. As extroverts from large families, we got excited about huge, holiday parties. Fortunately for us, almost every weekend at Oak Park was a party, with Mexican Banda music blasting tuba beats or Cambodian kids break dancing in the apartment above us. Most of all, we both wanted to take part in a ministry of compassion and social justice, in which we would serve people by living alongside them. Just as Jesus the Word came and made his dwelling among us, we hoped to bear his presence in our neighborhood.

Dan took seriously Jesus' command to take no extra bag, purse, or sandals that could weigh him down. Instead, he was focused on the mission to go where Jesus was going. Freed from chasing upward mobility or a lifestyle comparable to his suburban peers, Dan spent his time listening to God and doing his will. He lived simply, as he resided in the same conditions and on the same budget of those around him, and he trusted in God's provision. His lifestyle not only freed him from stress and covetousness, but also enabled him to walk humbly while loving mercy and doing justice. As we both made our dwelling among our neighbors at Oak Park, we soon came to see their needs and the forces that shaped them.

Cultivating a Ministry of Presence

When I first arrived in Oakland in the early 1990s, youth gangs dominated our neighborhood. They made sense to me. If you faced threats from physical harm, and the police and other adults weren't around to assist you, then you needed the backup from friends.

The largest gangs in Oakland were the Crips. Surprisingly to some, though, these Crips who claimed the color blue were Cambodian gangsters: the Oaktown Crips (OTC) and the next generation, Oaktown Junior Crips (OJC). Related to them were other Southeast Asian youth gangs, the Oakland Mien Crips (OMC) and the Oakland Mien Boys (OMB). The graffiti tags that claimed their turf were ubiquitous. Bored kids would even use White-Out correction fluid to paint the initials of gangs on Oak Park's balcony railings.

These youth, most of whom were born in refugee camps and resettled to Oakland when they were very young, quickly assimilated to their new environment. However, they didn't acculturate into middle-class, white America. They entered urban underclass neighborhoods spawning oppositional culture, a response to blocked opportunities. Gangs flaunted their quick money and street power, and the little kids emulated them.

A year after I moved into Oak Park, I noticed some Oak Park third-graders using chalk to graffiti "OJC" on the sidewalk in front of the corner store.

"That's sorta' weak," I commented a bit disdainfully when I looked at the sidewalk chalk graffiti.

"Well, can you help us start a gang?" Samath asked hopefully. Being the original gangster (OG) poser that I was, I shared my street knowledge as an OG.

"First, you've got to quit using chalk. Second, you've got to gather your homies."

"So can you help us?" he pleaded.

"No, but I can ask Dan to meet with you."

And that was the ignoble beginning of the Boyz Group, a group of Oak Park boys and their friends who met weekly for Bible study, prayer, and hijinks. When Samath asked Dan to start the gang, Dan exacted some conditions. He said that gangs tagged graffiti, but this group would clean up graffiti. Gang members often dropped out from school, but the boys in this gang had to try to stay in school. Finally, if they wanted Dan to drive them around, they had to study the Bible, and then Dan would take them places. The boys quickly agreed, motivated especially by the free rides.

Dan and Rob Swift, a Christian from U.C. Berkeley who had moved in with us, began bringing the boys to Harbor House on Friday nights. The original moniker for the group, "Peace, No Gangsters" didn't catch, so the incipient gang became known simply as Boyz Group. This group for mentoring and Bible study became so tight and valued that it ran for over sixteen years, with about three generations of different cohorts. Older boys would bring their younger brothers, who would then mentor their even younger cousins.

Carlos Flores, another UC Berkeley college grad, became the longest-serving and most faithful leader. He gathered the group weekly and hung out with the guys for over fifteen years! Raised in a conservative, Mexican American Assemblies of God church in California's Central Valley, he was an only child, chubby and fearful. College brought him out of his shell and introduced him to new types of ministry and a new lifestyle when he became heavily involved with InterVarsity Christian Fellowship. At their conferences and large group meetings, he felt called to make life choices in service of others.

One InterVarsity alumni conference cemented his desire to move into a low-income neighborhood. The speaker, Tom Sine, spoke on future trends—such as growing global urbanization—and how Christians might join in God's movement in the world. Interestingly, Dan, Rob, and I attended that conference as well, not knowing the group of UC Berkeley alumni that included Carlos. Sine shared a holistic theology of mission that integrates values of social justice with an orientation for evangelism. A few of those Cal alumni moved into Harbor House's neighborhood, where they began a fellowship that Dan and Rob joined. Carlos met us through this fellowship. He was searching for a Christian community where he could serve the poor and develop his faith.

When his parents retired to Mexico and left the Central Valley, Carlos moved in with us at Oak Park and the four of us shared the tiny one-bedroom apartment for a spell. Almost immediately, Carlos began to help lead the Boyz Group, driving the kids to Harbor House, studying Scripture, and playing basketball and pool with them afterward. Noting the powerful influence of gang life in our community, Carlos explained, "Part of the purpose [of the group] was to keep them out of trouble and off the streets—we gave them a place to go."

The Cambodian middle school students quickly made the group into something that functioned like a gang, as it gave them identity and community. While the sports gave them a healthy outlet for fun, the sessions of sharing built strong brotherhood and connection. Carlos accounted for the popularity and longevity of the group to the comfort that was established among the adults and youth: "The big thing was having a safe space. By that, I mean somewhere where they could be free to talk. When the group was going well, the boys were doing the majority of the talking. I had a strong interest in how they were doing, and it was really a non-judgmental atmosphere. And when you model it—not judging— they learned to act the same way."

Whereas most urban youth develop a tough, reticent, street attitude in response to their circumstances, these young men gained different coping skills. They came to share openly what they went through, and they learned to offer support to one another's struggles. Carlos would close meetings by praying for them, and eventually they took turns praying for one another as well.

Dan, Rob, and Carlos provided alternative role models for the youth in dealing with their violent setting. One evening, Carlos encountered the boys walking down the street carrying baseball bats. Carlos suspected that they didn't need so many bats to play at night, and he was right. One of them had just been jumped, and they were out to retaliate. Instead, Carlos rounded them up in his car and took them to Harbor House. "We talked about how to respond to someone in peace," Carlos shared, "so the fight didn't escalate. This was a good example of what would have happened if we hadn't had Boyz Group. They would have followed what they learned on the streets and gotten into trouble."

Carlos found what he was searching for after college: a place where he could hang out with friends, a group of guys that he could ball with, and a community that he could serve. He found a hospitable home at Oak Park, and his availability—to God and to others—became his faithful ministry of time and presence.

In spite of their dangerous surroundings, the members of the Boyz Group themselves became people of peace. Very few of the core members joined gangs or had dealings with the police. In stark contrast, those at Oak Park who didn't join Boyz Group got into trouble. Rival gangs often have shot at them, and they now have police records. But God didn't just protect the Boyz Group from physical violence. He also led them and others to spiritual peace.

Peace from Street Life

One member of the Boyz Group, Veasna, eventually became a leader of the group. Always with a wide grin on his face, Veasna lived at Oak Park as a young child. After moving into public housing in North Oakland, he would return to visit cousins on both sides of his family. When he started high school, he couldn't help but face hassles from rival gangs, of all racial backgrounds, on the streets. "They out there," he intoned gravely. "You bump into people and they don't like you, then you get in trouble." To get protection, and also to have some fun, Veasna jumped into a gang, Cambodian Pilipino Crips (CPC).

Like other youth gangs claiming a color, CPC members spent most of their waking time together on the streets. Their days consisted of chilling with weed, punctuated by the quick thrills of committing petty crimes. Veasna recalled, "Being around them, it was always jacking cars, robbing houses, doing drugs. They hang all-nighters, smoke a lot of weed. Whenever my friend had a car, we'd drive everywhere, two cars deep, go all night. That's why I was tired a lot."

Before he got in too deep with the gang, Veasna got a job with Harbor House's Youth Employment Program. A year later, he joined the Boyz Group that met at Harbor House. "After I joined the Boyz

Group," remembered Veasna, "I got close to them. The group helped me think more, care more, pray more." Here he was among young men like himself, but they were making different choices.

One of Veasna's big choices was whether to stay in CPC or not. When he was with his crew, like many gang members, he acted out with bravado. When he was with you by himself, he acted less self-assuredly but also more thoughtfully—like many gang members when you catch them alone. He decided that the violence he lived through wasn't going to end unless he did something. He observed, "I wanted to be with my crew, but when I saw what they did, I feel I didn't want to do those things. Street life, it's all about retaliation. The only way to stop it is to step away."

That choice to move away from the gang life and start working full-time has had lifelong consequences for Veasna. He explained that for his friends who scattered and joined other gangs, "It got a lot worse." Some were arrested, and some are hard-core cocaine addicts. Veasna noted, "The other day, I bumped into a friend, and he does crazy drugs. He's into cocaine, and now he gave up his life for it." Others are always on the watch for enemies fighting over turf. "Everybody around me has a gun. They all have guns now," Veasna somberly informed me. "Big guns, small guns. Like they say, they'd rather be caught with it than without it."

Peace from Spiritual Attacks

The other choice Veasna made was to become a Christian. Cambodians, who traditionally are Buddhist, wear spirit strings around their wrists, necks, and waists for protection from evil spirits. This protection is quite necessary. Like the gangs, spirits were also all around us at Oak Parks. I had my own bewildering brushes with spirits, which cemented my postmodern thinking about what constitutes ultimate reality.

Once, Oak Park kids came running to my apartment to summon me: "Wanna see a ghost dance?"

Having no idea what they were talking about and never having seen a dancing ghost before—or even a standing ghost—I followed them upstairs. At the home of the Khmer native healer, Bech Chuom, about a dozen youth stood crowded around his front window. I peered in, and I saw the ghost dance. Inside, a young teenager, Sarah, was by herself dancing to no music. Her hands, bent at the wrists, waved about slowly and fluidly, like the arms of sea anemone gently swaying in the currents.

That evening, the girl's mom pressed me to drive her and Sarah to Long Beach. The mother explained that they had to get a headdress to offer to the spirit who was now possessing her daughter. Evidently, Sarah wasn't doing the ghost dance. The ghost inside her was the one doing the dancing.

I immediately protested and said I couldn't drive her so far from Oakland. I wanted to back off while crossing my fingers in the sign of a cross, but that would be culturally rude. Besides, that trick only works for vampires. Having no experience exorcising demons, I wanted to avoid this spooky situation altogether.

At six the next morning, however, Sarah's mom showed up at my door and said, "Time to go!" Something must have gotten lost in translation. I had expressed my unbelief in the efficacy of the headdress offering, but they really wanted to get rid of the ghost.

In fact, the entire family showed up for the ride to Long Beach: Sarah the possessed; her mom and younger sister; her paraplegic father, who had been paralyzed by a land mine explosion; her grandmother; and Bech Chuom, who brought along a boom box to play Buddhist chants to keep the ghost at bay. I didn't feel I could say no to the family, especially the grandma and disabled father, who rarely went out. Sarah, all this time, had been staring blankly and didn't respond to any of our conversations.

Reluctantly, I borrowed a van and we were off. About halfway, along I-5 near Los Banos, Sarah's mom told me to get the girls and myself some lunch at McDonald's. When I returned with the Big Macs, the family had spread out a mat on the parking lot and began eating rice they had brought. Bech Chuom, dressed in his orange saffron robe, had taken out the boom box to continue blasting the chants. Meanwhile, some local rednecks in cowboy hats parked their trucks—complete with gun racks and NRA stickers—beside us. If they had known that besides the bald dude with the orange sash, the wheelchair guy in a skirt (really, a sarong), and the grandma eating little gobs of rice from an ornate, silver rice bowl caddy, there was a spirit-filled girl squatting on the ground with us, they probably would have stared even longer and more intently than the minute-long, fixed gazes they already gave us.

We made it to Long Beach, purchased the headdress, and promptly drove back to Oakland, a fourteen-hour round-trip drive. The next day, Sarah was back to her sweet self again. I asked her if she recalled anything, but she couldn't remember any of the entire last week's events.

The next week, I spoke to a counselor at Asian Community Mental Health Services about spirit possession. She nonchalantly replied, "Oh, yes, we see that a lot. She may have been recently abused." When refugee youth face traumatic experiences, she explained further, they often disassociate from the experience and act in culturally scripted ways.

Was Sarah abused, the explanation given by Western psychologists, or was she really possessed by a spirit, the attribution made by my Cambodian neighbors?

I would answer, yes. At Oak Park, I saw a few incidents of both abuse and of spirit activity. Both were plausible factors affecting how kids behaved. Even Carl once claimed to see a spirit coming out of a wall at a friend's Oak Park apartment.

Our neighbors' belief in spirits and their activity in our world was strong and shaped their day-to-day conduct. Families visited Bech Chuom regularly to consult about bouts of illness and bad luck, and he would make little dough figures aimed to confuse and draw the evil spirits away from real persons. Almost every Cambodian wore some sort of blessed spirit string for protection. Veasna's brother claimed that his spirit string saved his life when he got shot at and the bullet just missed him.

After praying about his life, Veasna decided to cut off his spirit string. He explained, "I feel God is my protection. When it's my time to go, he'll take me. I don't need a bracelet to follow the right path in life."

Similarly, after participating in a Bible study for a period, an Oak

Park mother took down the shrines in her home without any of the Christians prompting her to do so. She smiled and rationalized, "Jesus is more powerful than any spirit or shrine." Allayed of her fear of spirits, she truly did feel liberated and at peace.

For this peace and for its positivity in his life, Veasna continues to appreciate the role of Boyz Group. "Around with my homies, I don't feel safe. It's gonna go bad, and we gonna be in jail, or dead," he claimed. He then joked about a worse fate: "Or we be thirty years old and living with mom." In contrast, he chose another way: "Being around positive people, talking one on one [at the Boyz Group], helped me be a better person. It gave me a heart I never had—to be a caring person." Veasna's heart—shining through his broad, grinning smile—is that of a person who has found peace away from the streets and from the spirits.

Giving Voice to the Voiceless

When the Cambodian parents at Oak Park saw us assisting their children, they asked Dan and me to teach them English. Glad to offer our services, we began meeting in our living room twice a week. Eventually, we received a grant from a family literacy program from the Oakland Unified School District to teach from our home. The thinking behind the program was that if immigrant children observed their parents learning, the students would have role models and motivation to study hard as well.

This English as a Second Language (ESL) family literacy class seemed like a good idea to promote parent engagement in their children's education. Asian Community Mental Health Services even got contracted to host parenting classes in our apartment classroom. They sent consultants to our class to teach American parenting techniques of good communication.

Of course, the best laid plans often get waylaid. The consultants showed a video of refugee parents learning that their teenage daughter had become pregnant out of wedlock. The father in the video grew angry and disowned the girl. The mother was supposed to be the positive role model; she took the time to listen compassionately to the daughter's circumstances. The consultants hoped that the tearful reconciliation between mother and daughter would move viewers to nurture and share with their children. Yet when asked which parent responded well, the Cambodian moms in our class uniformly expressed their support of the father's actions. They expressed with consternation, "American are too free."

The consultants reinforced the idea that parents need to talk to their children. One mother complained, "I do talk." She paused for dramatic effect, then delivered her conclusion. "I tell them all the time to do this or to do that," she claimed. "They just don't listen!" Privately, I took whimsical pleasure in watching the Cambodian moms resist Americanization to the befuddlement of the consultants.

Despite our general ineffectiveness in teaching English, cultivating American parenting norms, or encouraging citizenship, these classes continued for years—similar to the Boyz Group—because we hosts and guests bonded so closely. We continued having the classes because they were fun; we chatted, practiced English, drank coffee, and ate leftover donuts from Cambodian donut shops. Our activities weren't formal programs or ministries, but were more like spaces where moms could get a break from their shrieking kids.

We became so much a part of our neighbors' lives that Dan, Rob, Carlos, and I were soon invited to Oak Park weddings, Cambodian New Year Festivals at the Buddhist temple, and graduation parties. I taught some moms how to drive, and Rob felt comfortable enough to take naps at our neighbors' apartments, even when his apartment was just a few doors away.

Sylvia was the one Latina mom who joined our ESL class. She had grown up in Oaxaca, Mexico, where her father raised her to help the community. A disciplined student, Sylvia had graduated from university and worked as a public health nurse. Her parents split up, however, and her mother moved to Los Angeles. When visiting her mother, the mother's boyfriend assaulted Sylvia. To Sylvia's shock, her mother sided with her boyfriend and kicked Sylvia out. In just one month, Sylvia found herself alone in a new country without any financial support or English language skills. She then got together with Orlando, a Guatemalan construction worker.

Though a university graduate, Sylvia could only get piecework at a garment factory. She received one cent for each item she sewed and earned only ten dollars a day. Unable to survive on these scandalous wages, she and Orlando moved to Oakland and into Oak Park in 1994.

Just as Dan and I were welcomed by our refugee neighbors, Sylvia and her two-year-old daughter, Karina, received their hospitality as well. Karina became one of the glue kids who held our community together and to whom everyone was attached. "We lived at Oak Park for three years," Sylvia pleasantly reminisced, "and every day, kids would come and knock on her door to play with Karina." During Halloween, we routinely escorted dozens of Oak Park kids to go trick-or-treating. We drove outside our neighborhood to better hunting grounds in middle-class areas, where the children would charge madly from door to door. Getting free stuff from the rich was as exhilarating to me as it was for the kids. At the center and fully in the mix was little Karina, adorably dressed up as a little bee.

Although they loved the Oak Park community, severe water leaks in their apartment forced Orlando and Sylvia to move out. Over time, Orlando's problem with alcohol grew worse, and he would be absent for long periods of time. To support herself and Karina, Sylvia began cleaning twelve hours a day, seven days a week. She would get up at 5:00 a.m. to clean offices before workers showed up at 9:00 a.m. Then she would work at private homes during the day and return to clean other offices until midnight. Like many children of the working poor, Karina had to grow up without much parental supervision or care. "When I returned home at night, Karina was already asleep. When I left in the morning, she was still sleeping," Sylvia recalled. She bemoaned, "Karina begged me to spend just one day with her."

Even when she got pregnant again, Sylvia continued working until her delivery date. She hid her condition from her employers so she wouldn't get fired. Although she needed the wages, the toll of long hours of physical labor put her life, as well as the life of her baby, at great risk. Sylvia already suffered from high blood pressure and diabetes, and during the baby's delivery, which required a cesarean section, she went into cardiac arrest.

Fortunately, both Sylvia and the baby, Daniella, survived.

To survive financially, Sylvia returned to work as soon as she could after recovering from childbirth. Orlando, in the meantime, became even more physically abusive and threatening. His mother moved in, complicating matters, and also began fighting with Sylvia. Sylvia realized she had to do something to protect her daughters.

Even though she had lived in Oakland for twelve years, Sylvia had made few friends on which she could rely, because she worked so much. She had seen Dan in the neighborhood from time to time and remembered how he always took the time to ask how she was doing. So she went to look for him at Oak Park. She recalled Dan's strong presence in the community: "Of course, Dan was there!" Then, she shared gratefully about how he responded to her situation. She recounted, "After I told him everything, he got really mad and asked me why I took so long to seek help. Dan referred me to three places, one of them being Mujeres Unidos y Activas [MUA—Women United and Active]."

Sylvia, Karina, and baby Daniella moved out immediately and began a new life of recovery and activism. Through meetings and training with MUA and other organizations, Sylvia regained her self-esteem. Not only did she obtain life skills through MUA, but she soon became a leader who helped others in similar situations. Eventually, Sylvia became president of the board of MUA and participated in its organizing campaigns.

One of the organization's efforts is lobbying for legislation that secures a "Bill of Rights for Domestic Workers." Speaking from her own experiences, Sylvia insists, "We want to value and recognize the work we women do inside and outside the home." Recalling the unfair, long hours that she had to work, she advocates for basic worker rights: "The least we could do for mothers is to help women get their breaks and time for sleep."

Another issue that personally affects Sylvia and our Oak Park neighbors is immigration reform. As an undocumented immigrant, Sylvia has seen many other women separated from their families due to harsh deportation policies. In response, she joined a group traveling to Washington, DC, for a congress on the undocumented. While there, she was challenged to really stand for her cause.

Sylvia's group was to attend a hearing where the U.S. Secretary of Homeland Security was present. Along with other groups from across the nation, her organization wanted to shed light on the unconscionable American practice of splitting apart families and deporting them. To raise awareness, she was asked to hold up a banner.

By simply hoisting a sign, Sylvia could be arrested, deported, and she herself separated from her two daughters. In advance, she had prepared for this very scenario and told her daughters that if she were to be deported, they were to fly to Mexico and meet her, where she would join up with other deportees.

In spite of these enormous risks, Sylvia looked around at the others and decided, "We're not going to be silent anymore." At a U.S. Senate hearing on immigration in 2013, she and her fellow undocumented activists made their voices heard.

"No more deportations!" they chanted. Expecting only to be removed from the proceedings, Sylvia was actually arrested and detained in a cell with four women. She was not released until a day later.

Later that year, students at San Francisco State University organized an educational forum on immigration reform. To my surprise, Sylvia, whom I hadn't seen in a decade, was featured as one of the main panelists. When I heard her declare to the large audience, "I am undocumented and unafraid!" I was stunned by her transformation. She had been healed and redeemed. From being a victim of wage theft, she now advocates for working mothers throughout the state. Formerly domestically abused and left homeless, Sylvia today has the boldness to challenge injustice. Once barely able to hold an English conversation in our ESL classes, she raises her voice in Washington, DC, and speaks for all immigrants.

As a guest to an amazing performance, I gave her a standing ovation. Even though I am a college professor and she is a janitor, we have a lot in common. My ancestors had to work long hours and scratch by to make a living, only to lose everything because of racism and xenophobia. My grandfather and his children had to live in the shadows simply because he didn't have the right papers. My mother's siblings were torn apart as government policy failed to support family values. Sylvia and I are both from Oak Park, home to immigrant families trying desperately to make a home.

Through our ESL class and Dan's timely intervention, we were able to witness the transformation of another person of peace. Sylvia is now a person promoting peace and justice, speaking for me as well.

The Recovery of Sight for the Blind

The other program initiated by Oak Park tenants, in addition to the Boyz Group and ESL, was a tutoring club. Since their parents could not help them much with homework in English, the youth asked for school help. And since they were so darn cute, we couldn't help but try to support them. For myself, doing structured activities with kids is frustrating. I feel it's like training squirrels to sit still and do tax paperwork. That's why I didn't really want to lead the Boyz Group, and why I didn't want to tutor. I got too impatient with the students and would give them their answers just to get it over and be done with it.

At the same time that Carlos joined our Christian community at Oak Park, fellow UC Berkeley alumni from InterVarsity Christian Fellowship (IVCF) also moved into the complex. Alice Wu, Christine Ma, and Mae Chan were all interested in doing urban ministry. Already sensitive to issues of inequality and suffering, Mae explained, "IVCF had messages about loving Jesus through community and giving away your money. Going into college, I was already looking for the deeper meaning. I wondered, 'God, where are you in the world, and how can you let people suffer?'"

Mae's initial impression of Oak Park would have been daunting to most. The summer of 1994, Dan and I were organizing to get rid of the rampant drug dealing at Oak Park. We wrote down the license plates of all the cars that visited and reported them regularly, along with the description of the drug dealers, to the police drug hotline. The drug dealers responded by slashing our car tires and physically threatening Dan. Dan even moved out temporarily because of fears for his safety.

Dan returned to host Alice and Mae for dinner when they wanted to take a tour of Oak Park. We had been praying for some women to come help, because the Oak Park girls wanted a discipleship group like the boys had. We also had been praying for some women to marry, but that's another chapter.

Mae recalls, "What I remember is that feeling that we were in a foreign land. The buildings were super run down. It was the real ghetto, which I only had heard about." When our meal was over and Dan wanted to drive back to where he was staying, our guests had to escort Dan in order to protect him from the drug dealers.

Dan's predicament left Mae incredulous, as she described: "We walked out with Dan, like we were his human shield. We walked slowly, all of us around Dan, to get to his car. Dan had to go, so we all had to go with him."

Despite the perils of our neighborhood, Mae and Alice moved in and immediately began relating to the youth. The kids asked for help in school so we initiated weekly tutoring sessions. Mae described how receptive the kids were to our attention, and how useful they made us feel: "Tutoring was the structured thing I did most. It was at our apartment sometimes and just crazy—kids everywhere, covering every bit of the carpet. They just wanted a place to be. They appreciated our help, and they knew that's what we were there for. It felt so, 'I can be helpful.'"

These little promoters of peace certainly welcomed us, especially by making tutors feel needed and useful. That's an enormous gift. Then again, the kids didn't always create a peaceful calm.

Like our volunteer work in hosting ESL, we weren't really trained to teach or tutor effectively. Instead, we developed curriculum and organized activities according to our own creativity and whims. Mae conveyed, "A lot of times, tutoring would break down to total chaos. That's where I learned about the game—the sleeping game. 'Let's pretend to be asleep, where everyone is quiet and has their eyes closed.'"

In fact, since we were each volunteering our time as neighbors, we didn't have to follow any set church policies, government guidelines, or foundation priorities. We came to call ourselves Oak Park Ministries (OPM), with our own motto: "Oak Park Ministries: Founded by mortal men, Led by God, Funded by no one." The lack of funding actually freed us to do whatever we wanted. Mae explained, "We were all learning together and open to trying anything. And we'd laugh if it was crazy and it didn't turn out. It was entrepreneurial. It was okay not to know."

To encourage the students, we rewarded them with small prizes and quarterly trips. If they attended tutoring regularly, they would get the chance to slide down something. In the summers we'd go to the waterslides, and in the winters we'd go sledding. We took so many of these trips, I decided to buy a minivan to transport the loads of families. Paradoxically, even though I was an unmarried graduate student in an urban slum, I became a suburban mom.

Other transformations also took place as we were guests at Oak Park. Children who couldn't read had their eyes opened to the wonders of books. Teenagers harassed by gangs and spirits were set free from fear. Moms who were mute in this society spoke truth to power.

These changes came about because our neighbors were people seeking peace. They were the ones who initiated each of the ministries at Oak Park—Boyz and Girlz Groups, ESL, and tutoring—and these groups lasted for years because of their own initiative. Our neighbors were never our projects, but our gracious hosts whose hospitality we sought to repay.

Lambs among Wolves

Certainly, not everyone is a person promoting peace, and we dealt with much disappointment and hurt caused by our fellow neighbors. Some youth did join gangs and become involved with crime, and others got pregnant too early and became a second generation of welfare recipients. Much of our lament draws from the wasted lives of those around us.

In 1996, Mae married Rick Frey and they moved into their own apartment at Oak Park. While they were away on vacation, though, some thieves broke in and stole about a thousand dollars in goods. Mae was most heartbroken over losing an heirloom ring from Rick's mother.

The thieves weren't stealthy professionals who left without a trace. They took the time to ransack and vandalize the apartment. Eggs and flour were hurled across the walls. "I remember our pictures, family photos, were on the ground and had egg on them," recounted Mae. She then reflected on how personally painful the crime was: "I think the robbery felt worse because it looked like the thieves had a good time doing it."

Beyond the theft of valuables and heirlooms, worse than the loss of one's sense of security within one's own home, and even more troubling than the fact that the robbers were having fun, was that Oak Park kids were involved. Kids would whisper they knew who did it, but the youth wouldn't say who. "I remember feeling betrayed," Mae added, "because of course, someone knew what had happened. I felt betrayed that people knew and didn't stop them. When I knew the kids weren't telling, I felt like we were outsiders."

After years of living with the youth, tutoring them, taking them on trips, and mentoring the young women's group, Mae felt unappreciated and violated. When the youth didn't reveal the identities of the vandals, Mae quite justifiably complained, "You would protect them over us?"

Reflecting on her ministry, she felt overwhelmed and questioned whether she was making a difference: "Oh, we're not saving anybody. It's like digging in the sand."

The gang of thieves broke into other apartments as well. They robbed the laptop of another Christian who had moved in, Cameron Cardona, and they stole the candy sales earnings of the grandmother, Khlot Ry. I was angered and embittered, too. After all that we had done for them, the kids let us down.

After a few days of sleuthing, we cracked the case. Taking a scene from the movie *LA Confidential,* Cameron and I played good cop, bad cop while singling out and interrogating individual Boyz Group members. We would fib and say, "Channouen said you were involved and know who did it. Tell us, Ken." Then Ken would snap under pressure and confess to what he knew. We'd then bring in the next kid and say, "Ken said you were involved and know who did it. Tell us, Sam." And likewise, Sam would wilt and spill his guts. Toppling like dominoes, they each came clean.

The main crew of thieves, who came from outside Oak Park, were arrested and put in a restorative justice program. They had to write apologies and repay the cost of the stolen goods. The Oak Park youth who were involved had only acted as look-outs. Apparently, they didn't want to snitch because they were afraid of the main crew. We made them apologize to Mae and Rick, and they also had to buy and serve turkeys for our Oak Park Thanksgiving party.

Even though they confessed and made restitution, I resented the kids for their selfish actions and their silence. I've asked Mae how she forgave the boys and continued to live at Oak Park after the incident. Having seen firsthand the limited opportunities and pervasive fear in the neighborhood, she responded, "These kids are in such a hard situation. They're young and in a hard place. How could they not make stupid choices given the choices they could see?"

I don't so easily extend grace as Mae, though. I think they make stupid choices because they're stupid. At least, they could take more personal responsibility for their actions.

Living among wolves takes grace, as well as realistic expectations. Not to say that these young men are wolves, but that Christians can be taken advantage of as they turn the other cheek. That's why Jesus cautioned his disciples when he sent them out as guests. That's what we learned the hard way.

Each of our neighbors faced incredible needs: overcoming wartime trauma, learning English, dealing with gangs and drug dealers, and lacking real work opportunities. As Mae concluded, our efforts were often like digging in the sand.

Sheep in Sustainable Pastures

Living among wolves, as we all are, requires that we stay close to the Shepherd and drink from the waters where he leads us. Despite our best efforts to mentor and tutor, none of the students in the Boyz Group graduated from high school during the first eight years of the group's existence. Although we taught English faithfully, only one or two refugee adults have maintained a job with a living wage. Instead, we saw cycles of violence, the protraction of poverty, and the intensification of inequality. These patterns were not just grim statistics that we read about, but the dire situation facing our friends—neighbors who had become like our family.

How did those of us who were Christians at Oak Park sustain ourselves? Sheep who wander off alone would easily be killed. One of the first relocating Christians once woke me up before 6:00 a.m. and announced, "Russell, you have to lend me five thousand dollars!"

"Get out of here!" I complained and tried to return to sleep.

"I need five thousand dollars!" he insisted. He had tried, on his own, to befriend the drug dealers and evangelize them. He loaned them money to get them to stop dealing drugs, but then they asked for more or else they'd harm his family. Although Dan and I warned him about the dangers of these dealers, he wouldn't listen and became too embroiled with them. Since I wouldn't give him the cash to extricate himself, he quickly moved out and had to return to the suburbs to escape.

For the most part, the Christians at Oak Park worked together, even though we attended four different evangelical churches. Each of these congregations prayed for our efforts at Oak Park while we aimed to be committed members to our home churches. Our membership within local congregations, where we would receive both support and accountability, was essential for Oak Park Ministries.

I continued to be a member at Grace Fellowship Community Church in San Francisco, worshiping there on Sunday, joining in Bible study on Thursday, and meeting with a discipleship group biweekly. Grace Fellowship was truly a home base for me, where I received great teaching and contemporary liturgies that fed my mind and heart. Oak Park was my mission field, where I aimed to witness God's grace and peace. The continual movement of being sent into the field, returning to base, and being sent again was like Jesus' sending of the apostles in Luke 10.

At the closing of each Sunday service, we received a benediction to love and serve the world. After a week at Oak Park, I would return to Grace Fellowship with either joy or lament. Jesus would then nourish me again with his words and sacrifice. Along with regular deep readings of Scripture, we would discuss books such as *Resident Aliens: Life in the Christian Colony* and *Restoring At-Risk Communities: Doing It Together.*[4] Weekly Communion became a significant ritual for me, as living at Oak Park exposed my vulnerability and weaknesses so tangibly that I felt hungry for Jesus' bread. Even if I did not know it at the time, regularly feeding from Scripture and the Eucharist sustained me.

Our routines kept us sane amidst our crazy busy lives as well. Rob needed the most help with structuring his schedule. In order for Rob to have time to teach ESL, we began cooking for him so that he wouldn't be eating wiener winks—toaster oven-baked hot dogs wrapped in bread and cheese—as his primary food source. He seemed to become revitalized after eating a healthy meal, so we initiated a cooking rotation for the ten college-educated Christians who came to live at Oak Park. One of us would cook dinner for the other nine, and then we would all come together to share a meal.

Our community meals, like my regular Bible study and worship times at Grace Fellowship, kept us going. It worked well because it cleared time for others to pray, tutor, teach ESL, or host mentoring groups. The meals had to be home-cooked and healthy, with at least some serving of vegetables. Since we didn't go out to eat, we saved money that could be used for tutoring trips and ESL dinners. It was amazingly convenient, too, because I only cooked two to three times a month, but got fed nightly.

In time, a red Tupperware plate, purchased from the Dollar Tree down the block, became the symbol of the OPM community. We didn't want to make the host wash so many dishes, so we each brought our own plate and cutlery. If we couldn't stay for the meal, we would drop off the plate and could retrieve a plateful of food later. OPM members may have had conflicts, but we were bonded by the Holy Spirit and dinners eaten off Tupperware.

Along with church and community rituals, each of us had our own personal practices that kept us from burning out as well. Dan has a rich prayer life, and I wrote hundreds of journal pages, repeating the same prayer requests time and time again. Carlos, Christine, and I trained for a marathon in 1994, and to this day I continue to drive fifteen minutes up to the Oakland hills, run, and recreate within the Lord's creation. When I reach the Tres Sendas trail, an hour's run deep into Redwood Regional Park, I am often caught keenly aware of God's presence. Whatever the season, I've run there and felt welcomed home.

When I am crushed by life in Oakland's flatlands, I heed the psalmist's refrain: "I lift up my eyes to the mountains. Where does my help come from? My help comes from the LORD, the Maker of heaven and earth" (Psalm 121:1–2). I run to the mountains, and the sight of his creation—his glory—restores me.

Because of these corporate and personal disciplines, I haven't really burnt out in Oakland. While I am overwhelmed by the needs, traumas, and struggles we each face, I have been sustained by God's presence among those around me.

Returning to Jesus with Joy

Along with these holy habits of church, fellowship, and Sabbath, we at OPM have found that the "joy of the LORD is your strength," as another restorer of cities, Nehemiah, had claimed (Neh. 8:10). Our ministry to be sent out and live among our neighbors very rarely saw astounding life-changing conversions or thorough-going community transformation. Most of the time we toiled on, attempting to be faithful and fruitful rather than successful. And like the authors of our faith, we didn't always see the fruits of our labor. In one case, though, we did return to Jesus with joy, feeling as if "even the demons submit to us in your name" (Luke 10:17).

Carl and his three younger siblings didn't have a very stable childhood. Their mother had a series of relationships, and each time she got a new boyfriend, they would move. When they moved to Oak Park, it was one of the few times Carl's mom had a steady job as a nursing assistant and lived alone with her kids.

As an African American young man, Carl felt that he could never be himself on the streets in Oakland. "In the twenties," he explained about the name of our neighborhood, "if you're black kid, you have to do the same thing: smoke and face peer pressure to be a bad kid." He loved to draw comic art, but his peers would deride him and knock his drawing pad to the ground. Carl complained of his confinement as a black kid in the ghetto: "They'd [other African American boys] try to steal your ambition; it was always frustrating. I was always labeled, 'You're trying to be something you're not.'"

Within Oak Park, however, Carl received the same welcome that Sylvia, Mae, and I received. For the first time, among the Cambodians and Latinos, he could be who he wanted and do what he wanted. He affirmed, "I always felt at home at Oak Park. I would have kids from Oak Park sit around me and watch me draw. No one interfered. I could draw, play baseball. At Oak Park, you could be yourself. Everyone felt like my brother and sister. I wasn't expected to do anything but be what I was."

Carl did well enough in track to obtain offers for college scholarships, but his mother wouldn't sign the acceptance papers. She wanted him to remain at home to watch his siblings. Once she got another boyfriend, though, he made the kids leave the house. Carl joined the Navy, but he had to be discharged a year later because of a medical problem.

Despite his talents, work ethic, and intelligence, Carl became homeless at the age of nineteen. He didn't lack personal responsibility, but he didn't have an opportunity to get ahead. After the Navy, he first went to stay with an aunt, but she was too ill to host him. For three nights, he slept in her apartment complex's laundry room. He would put in a few quarters in the dryers to warm up the room, and then lock himself in for the night. When that became arduous, he went back to Oak Park. He recalls, "I didn't go to stay there, but I knew people there—the only place I didn't have to be someone I wasn't. My initial thought was I could sleep in the parking lot."

Carl told Dan and me a story about being homeless due to a house fire, so we offered to let him stay in our living room for a few nights. A few nights turned into a few weeks, and then Carl found work at a local movie theater. He came and simply stayed, just as I had come initially for a few months and then stayed for years with Dan. A lot like the stray cats that came and stayed with Dan.

Learning from our Cambodian neighbors about how to be gracious hosts, we became hospitable to Carl. Perhaps most importantly, we took the time just to hang out. Carl confided to me that even though Dan had his own busy work schedule, he often stopped what he was doing to show Carl the ropes: "Dan had his own business, a cleaning business. It was the first time someone actually showed me how to clean house. We went to the Oakland Hills together, and I have a duster now, because of him."

As his hosts, we included Carl in all aspects of our shared life. The community dinners were the first time Carl chatted with others over a meal at home. He joined us on our runs and volunteered with us on political campaigns. Appreciating how we held things in common, he was struck by the generosity of the community: "I remember I used to be afraid to drive," he expressed. "No one ever would let me use a car, but Rob would let me use his car a lot. He had a Saturn and you had a white minivan. This was a lifestyle that I wanted, where friends trusted you."

About a year after joining us, Carl suddenly vanished. He took his belongings and disappeared, taking with him about a hundred dollars of bake sales which we had saved for tutoring trips. Although we were slightly miffed, we were more quizzical about why he left so abruptly. We carried on at Oak Park, counting Carl as another one in the statistics of Oakland's lost boys. Like any good host, we didn't expect to be paid back.

Then, ten years later, Carl did pay us back, more than we could hope.

He found me on Facebook and we reconnected. He apologized for what he had done and now that he was back on his feet, he wanted to reestablish ties.

Carl admitted that he left abruptly because he overheard Dan wondering with someone about Carl's future plans. He felt like a burden, and so he ran away to Las Vegas. Having learned to drive with Rob's car, Carl first got work as a taxi driver. Then, following the advice of a big-tipping cab passenger, he got all the free training he could get. He took advantage of financial aid and got his bachelor's degree in English at the University of Nevada, Las Vegas. Later, while working at Comcast, he made use of their corporate training programs and moved up within the corporation to become an IT specialist. He's now saving up to buy a home in the state of Washington.

More gratifying than hearing of Carl's career success is learning about who Carl has become. Having been homeless himself, Carl now acts as a gracious host and father. When his ex-wife couldn't care for her baby from another man, Carl stepped in immediately. He explained, "I know what it's like to have nowhere to go. I didn't want James to have nowhere to go." For two years, Carl raised this toddler. James still calls Carl his daddy to this day and Carl thinks of him as his own son.

Our reconciliation with Carl, twenty years in the making, has led us to return to Jesus with joy and declare, "Even the demons submit to our name!" Carl himself said he was saved from going a different path, one that could have easily led to the demons of poverty, gang affiliation, or drug addiction. Instead, he matured into a man of integrity who has become responsible for others.

Jesus then reminds us, "Do not rejoice that spirits submit to you, but that your names are written in heaven" (Luke 10:20). Actually, we of OPM didn't do much to make spirits submit. Rob napped on Kosal's couch. Mae and I drank coffee with Sylvia. Dan and Carlos drove kids around. We were just available and present to witness God at work. And because we were guests, we got the opportunities to rejoice with people of peace whose own lives were transformed. Some may not have become Christians, but quite a few chose to follow Jesus along with us!

The Humility of Guests and Hosts

I learned from my father that the Chinese virtue of humility is both an attitude and a practice. He warned me that from his experience, Chinese had to work twice as hard as whites to get the same pay. The maltreatment of Chinese in America shouldn't make us feel inferior, though. He taught that as long as we worked hard, we were capable of becoming whoever we wanted. At the same time, we are no better than anyone else, even if we become successful and others do not.

This attitude of modesty—that we're no worse or better than anyone else—translates into practices of service and respect. As the youngest child in my family, my job at Chinese banquets was to make sure that everyone's teacup was kept full. My dad, without fail, reminded me at these meals to be alert to the needs of others. I think he took as much pride in seeing me serve food to dinner guests as he did in seeing me get good grades. It seemed like every Chinese American kid received high marks on tests, but not every kid learned to serve others first.

The Chinese characters making up the words for humility, *qiang xun*, include both of these aspects. *Qiang* means to have a yielding spirit, not seeking one's own pride or recognition. It pictures someone speaking while holding shafts of grain together, suggesting that words of humility prioritize the unity and harmony of the group first. *Xun* is the pictograph of the way a grandchild walks. We are to see ourselves like children, moving and acting in deference to our wiser elders.

Unlike Americans, who value egalitarian relationships, the Chinese recognize the hierarchical nature of relationships that have uneven power dynamics. Since it is easy for those with power to become paternalistic or patronizing when they serve others, we must learn Christ's humility and self-emptying. As we fill our different roles, whether as a parent/child or guest/host, we need to fulfill our responsibilities with love and a humbleness to serve.

This Chinese understanding of humility serves as a helpful counterbalance to American approaches to urban ministry and development. As guests in any community, we need to approach our neighbors empty of expectations and plans. Instead, we must become reliant on the people of peace whom God sends our way. When we host ministries, we must be servants of others first, prioritizing their concerns over our own. The fact that we may have more education or more financial resources does not make us any better, but it does give us the responsibility to share generously and love unconditionally.

When doing ministry, our joy and strength cannot be based on our own success or power. We receive these gifts only when being guests of the King and recognizing our limitations while in exile.

CHAPTER 4

An Asian American
Dream for Justice

Like the Hakka who were constantly uprooted, Oak Park residents
had to search for a new home. In the spring of 1999, the City of
Oakland condemned our apartment complex as uninhabitable, and
rightly so. Health inspectors uncovered dozens of code violations,
including lack of heating, severe mold and rodent infestation, and leaky
roofs. One Cambodian grandmother, Touch Phan, had so many ceiling
leaks that she funneled rainwater through garbage liners into a 30-gallon
can in the middle of her living room. The dampness of her apartment
spawned mounds of maggots that crawled across her carpet. Our complex's plumbing system was so clogged that Alejandra, a single mother
of three, woke up to a fountain of sewage spurting out of her toilet.
The Littlevoices, a Native American family, perilously kept all four stove
burners lit during the night because they had no other heating.

To address these conditions, the Oak Park Tenants Association wrote
fact-filled letters and held angry meetings with the landlord's representatives. Still, no repairs were made. We then contacted city officials, who
responded with a comprehensive inspection that led to the condemnation of the buildings. In an amazing display of unity, we organized about

two hundred of our fellow tenants to file a housing lawsuit to bring the buildings up to code. At this point, the owners declared corporate bankruptcy, ensuring that no funds for repairs would come from the landlord. OPM members feared we had made a grave mistake in initiating the lawsuit in the first place.

Our beloved community was about to be torn apart.

Not only was Khlot Ry's apartment condemned, but the agency that issued her housing waiver ordered her to move. Quite justifiably, they would not pay rent for a substandard unit. However, at age seventy-seven, Grandmother Khlot refused to leave Oak Park. Having lost her husband and four sons during the Cambodian Civil War, she fled to escape the Khmer Rouge's genocide. Now facing another traumatizing forced relocation, she would rather lose her valuable housing subsidy than leave her remaining family and friends.

Alice Wu and I searched Oakland for buildings with multiple, vacant apartments in order to keep our community intact. This was during the dot.com boom, and high-tech workers from Silicon Valley, some forty miles away, were gentrifying even our part of Oakland. Our prospects were grim but surprisingly, we found one complex two miles from Oak Park with eighteen vacant units. The only lit apartment was inhabited by the owner's lonely son. This place might be the only location where Khlot Ry and the other elders might be able to stay close to their fellow Cambodians. But frankly, it gave me the heebie-jeebies. I felt as if I were entering the Bates Motel from the movie *Psycho*.

To a mixture of disappointment and relief, we soon learned that the Psycho apartments were not for rent. The owners planned to redevelop that entire complex. We remained stuck in our condemned building, almost like squatters in abandoned units.

The condemnation began our summer of prayer. OPM met daily in the early morning to plead that God would save our neighbors and ourselves. We needed to depend on the Spirit's strength, not on our own messianic strategies and our own trust in our personal connections to power. It was easy to rally against and target the landlords as the evil villains, but we knew we were to forgive and love them. We also were unclear as to what God's kingdom looked like in our case—what might entail the empowerment of our neighbors, the cultural and physical transformation of the community, or the advancement of the church? We could only pray and wait for answers.

The American Way of Justice

Justice, as understood typically in the United States, is the fair protection of one's rights and the correct use of power. Christians fighting to correct injustices, then, find themselves battling abuses of power. For example, founder and president of the International Justice Mission, Gary Haugen, writes that "injustice occurs when power is misused to take from others what God has given them, namely their life, dignity, liberty or the fruits of their love and labor."[1] Since injustice involves the strong preying on the weak, Christians need to defend the weak. We do so by using our gifts, resources, and power to rescue the weak and bring oppressors to justice.

Using the discourse of "victim rescue," Haugen writes that Christians need humility, courage, and righteous anger to go about the task of seeking justice. Like attorneys, we should collect evidence, do casework, and hold perpetrators accountable. Those who are unfairly treated can then secure justice when their rights and dignity are restored. In this way, Christians may employ the same logic and strategies of the secular world in order to gain power and to fight for justice. Haugen suggests a model of legal redress in gaining justice.

Another model is community organizing, by which "victims" organize themselves for power. In community-organizing campaigns modeled after Saul Alinsky's Industrial Areas Foundation and the United Farm Workers led by Dolores Huerta, Larry Itliong, and Cesar Chavez, organizers build solidarity around common, felt needs. They organize campaigns fueled by the "cold anger," the fierce motivation that drives community members to address their situation. To build the organization, the campaign only takes on concrete, winnable issues that will spur members to further organizing. Once a target is identified who can change conditions—usually an official or government leader—the community rallies to hold that target accountable.

Social change, therefore, is incremental and is seen as the development of community leaders and institutions that can take charge of the decisions that affect them. For instance, Dennis Jacobsen, in *Doing Justice: Congregations and Community Organizing*, explains that "Organizing draws people into community based upon common self-interest. Perhaps we work together to seek drug treatment funding or to improve public education, or to secure more jobs. Organizing needs to connect with these kinds of short-term self-interest if it hopes to get people involved for whom these issues are real concerns."[2]

These Western concerns for rescuing the weak from injustice and for the satisfying of our own felt needs are legitimate. Nonetheless, they fall short, I think, of God's much grander vision of peace, or shalom. This other perspective may be seen with Chinese eyes.

China often is criticized for its failure to secure religious and political freedoms for individuals, but this nation rebuts that the United States fails to provide peace and safety equitably to all its citizens. In one report, China's State Council highlighted the injustices of the United States. These issues include the increasing number of American women who are victims of domestic abuse and sexual assault, the high rate of gun violence, and the staggering income gap within the United States. China further charges the United States for infringing on other nations and waging wars more than any other nation since the end of the Cold War.[3]

In this report, China challenges America for failure in fulfilling its moral responsibilities to society. Justice is not simply the securement of rights and entitlements or procedural fairness in law, but is also about the overall well-being of others and oneself. Chinese following Confucian teachings value the development of a virtuous character, epitomized in the quality of *ren*—benevolence, empathy, and humaneness. According to the Confucian Analects, a person of ren takes *both* personal responsibility for his actions *and* corporate responsibility for others' welfare: "A young man should be filial within his home and respectful of elders when outside, should be careful and trustworthy, broadly caring for people at large, and should cleave to those who are ren."[4]

This Chinese orientation to social justice as corporate responsibility is similar to the Old Testament prophetic tradition's call for shalom—a universal flourishing, wholeness, and well-being. As Isaiah described, God's kingdom of peace (shalom) results from justice: "The fruit of that righteousness will be peace; its effect will be quietness and confidence forever. My people will live in peaceful dwelling places, in secure homes, in undisturbed places of rest" (Isa. 32:17–18). Justice and righteousness lead to stable relations of peace and concrete situations of security.

Doing justice at Oak Park was our attempt to live out God's shalom in our neighborhood. Facing atrocious living conditions, we obviously wanted to correct the injustices our neighbors faced. We also wanted to hold our landlords, who were quite wealthy and powerful, accountable for providing decent housing. Yet more than simply correcting injustice, we aimed for our community's shalom on all of us, for all of us. With our refugee and immigrant neighbors, we longed for a secure place to rest together.[5]

Racial Reconciliation over Cambodian New Year

The Christians of Oak Park Ministries did not build the community at Oak Park, but we entered an apartment complex already tight with close relational networks. Once a few, key families received us, meeting other households was fairly easy, especially since people hung out a lot outdoors. After a few years of living among our neighbors and gaining more trust, OPMers began to take leadership around certain issues long before our lawsuit.

One of our main concerns, especially since OPMers found ourselves caught in the middle, consisted of the racial conflict between our Cambodian and Latino neighbors. As described previously, minor conflicts between children easily escalated into physical fights and gun violence in Oakland. Influenced by John Perkins and his Christian Community Development Association, OPMers strongly identified racial reconciliation as a sign of Jesus' good news, that groups would be united. Just as Jesus broke down the dividing wall between Jews and Gentiles, we felt that our faith should promote peace in a city divided by language, ethnicity, and race. Because of its poverty and lack of opportunities, our neighborhood had its fair share of angry persons in close proximity. Not only did they take out their anger within their homes in the form of domestic violence, but they also lashed out at others who spoke or looked differently from them.

Racial conflicts often arose over use of common areas. Oak Park, as the home of the largest concentration of Cambodians in Oakland, became the region's central festival site for Cambodian New Year. During the community's most important holiday, over five hundred people would gather at Oak Park to greet relatives and friends, sing karaoke, and play *Klah Klok*, a dice game where you could double or triple your bets. In the courtyard, boys and girls would line up opposite one another to compete in *Chol Chhoung*, a tossing contest in which losers would have to dance for the winners. Keo, who grew up at Oak Park with her three brothers and sister, remembers chasing others with water balloons and shaving cream. "That's our Khmer way of washing away the bad luck," she explained. I loved watching the grandmothers launching water balloons from second floor balconies to "bless" and douse their little ones.

At nightfall, someone would place a bouquet of flowers in the middle of the courtyard, and people would form a circle to dance around the flowers. With a huge speaker blaring Khmer music, one hundred of us would sway rhythmically forward and backward, with our palms cocked upward waving to the music. Joining the dance line was easy, even for someone with stiff joints like me, as dancers ranging from toddlers to grandmothers made room for everyone. As Keo recalled, Cambodian New Year was the most anticipated event of the year at Oak Park.

However, just as the games, food, and dancing became traditions, so did the drinking and ensuing late-night mayhem. Inevitably, someone would imbibe too much and start a fight. One year, the Oakland Police Department had to send helicopters to disperse a brawl in the parking lot. Another year, Latinos threw beer bottles at noisy Cambodians, which led to the stabbing of a Latino man.

To prevent these annual, miserable endings to Cambodian New Year, we discussed with the ESL students how we could improve relationships between neighbors. That year, the Cambodian mothers decided to host dinner for everyone, not just their friends and family. They cooked mounds of fried rice, stirred up large potfuls of papaya salad, and barbequed hundreds of beef satay sticks for the entire apartment complex. Rather than playing only Cambodian music, they interspersed Mexican songs for dancing. Every fourth song—to the delight of the kids—was the Macarena, to which even the grandmas knew the moves. We had rows of Oak Park tenants, six lines deep and twenty people long, swiveling late into the night. When you idiotically have your hands on your hips and you're jumping side to side in sync with your neighbor, it's tough to get into a fight with them.

Developing friendships across ethnic lines through food and dance was easy. These communal efforts not only reduced racial fear and animosity, but promoted interethnic friendships. Both Sylvia and Alejandra, moms at Oak Park, recounted how well the groups got along despite the language barriers. We even had some Romeo and Juliet, *Westside Story*-type romances between Cambodian and Latino teens. By sharing meals and partying together, our common life built the bonds that would later prove useful in taking collective action for other issues.

Surveilling the Police

The violence in Oakland wasn't just perpetrated in homes and on streets by civilians; Oakland police also had to use force—and sometimes, too much force—to suppress violent behaviors and to control groups. One time during the school year, a fight broke out between an Asian and a Latino middle school student at a school where the Oak Park youth attended. As they often do, the kids crowded in excitement to watch the action.

When the police arrived, they separated the Asians from the Latinos and made the boys kneel with their hands behind their necks, heads bowed. Some youth protested that they hadn't been involved, but the police yelled at them to shut up. The cops confiscated the kids' beanies and, in search of gang tattoos, commanded them to bare their chests. When a youth happened to look up, he'd be slapped on the back of the head to look at the sidewalk again.

The department's Asian Gang Taskforce then arrived and took head-shot photos of the Oak Park boys. These profile shots were for a gang database. If anyone in the database were ever to be arrested, he would be subject to harsher punishments.

When the Oak Park parents heard about the incident, they were mortified. In Cambodia, at the Tuol Sleng execution site, thousands of prisoners of the Khmer Rouge were photographed. The prisoners were forced to make autobiographical confessions, and then the majority were slaughtered. These photos still line the prison's walls today.

Having their children photographed by the government triggered traumatic memories for the parents. Like those arrested by the Khmer Rouge, their children were innocent. They were simply in the wrong place at the wrong time.

The ESL class became a forum for the parents to air their grievances again, and we listened to their fears. The parents complained that their children were not in gangs, so they didn't deserve to be racially profiled, presumed guilty, and placed in a gang database. One youth, Ras, always displayed a gentle spirit as he lovingly raised pets of all kinds. Agreeable and unassuming, he could easily play the part of a placid, young monk. Yet he was considered a gang member too, simply because he was Cambodian in a city with large, Southeast Asian gangs.

At the request of the parents, we contacted the police department about their practices, but we got no response. I then had to seek help from an attorney who worked for the American Civil Liberties Union in San Francisco. That lawyer sent the Asian Gang Task Force a letter, and requested a meeting for the parents. That letter garnered much more attention and the police agreed to come.

When the sergeant of the Task Force arrived at our apartment, he was met by a large contingent of concerned parents. He presented a slide show about the dangers of gang involvement, which the parents politely viewed. But when he spoke about their efforts to monitor gangs through the database of photographs, the parents spoke out in alarm. They protested that their sons had done no wrong, so their photos didn't need to be kept. By the end of the meeting, the sergeant relented. He agreed, albeit reluctantly, to return the photos.

This small victory proved we could confront injustice when working in concert. Although our community was poor in income, we were rich in social capital, that is, strong networks of trust and reciprocity. Utilizing bonding social capital, we mobilized groups of co-ethnics who faced the same racial profiling and institutional discrimination to work together. We then relied upon our bridging social capital, the connections we OPMers had with police officials and attorneys, to draw upon these outside resources to assist our community. This battle prepared us for our next organizing effort, this time a national issue over the culture wars.

Welfare Reform
and Corporate Irresponsibility

In 1992, President Bill Clinton won election with a promise to end welfare as we knew it. Portraying low-income mothers as lazy welfare queens, reformers argued that these women needed to be personally responsible for earning their benefits. The "Personal Responsibility and Work Opportunities Act of 1996" aimed to curtail welfare benefits to five years and to implement a workfare program. In the same line of argument, reformers complained that too many immigrants were cheating the welfare system and coming to the United States as leeches.

This proposed law also excluded non-citizens from receiving welfare, food stamps, and disability benefits. The news of this legislation had a huge, chilling effect at Oak Park. Every Cambodian family had someone receiving some form of welfare.

"I am old. My arms are weak. There is nothing I can do anymore. If I do not receive the help, I will starve and die," Bech Chuom grieved as he spoke to a *New York Times* reporter about the proposed welfare cut.[6] At age seventy-two, Bech Chuom was a shamanist healer who treated people who had sicknesses, troubles, and general bad luck. With elaborate tattoos on his chest and running down his arms, a shaved head, and colorful orange robes, he looked like a traditional Oriental monk in a quiet monastery. But instead, he lived among Latino day-laborers and a Chinese American graduate student, who would bring his UC Berkeley students for tours of Bech Chuom's huge shrine, which filled up his entire bedroom. One time, I brought an injured Cal Bear football player who asked for healing. Bech Chuom gladly said a few chants and then sipped some water. To my shock, he then spewed spit over the player's neck. I feared the lineman might blitz and tackle the healer.

Fortunately, the Bear player didn't flinch. He later told me, "I'd never put up with anyone spitting on me in a game, but I had to respect this elder."

Since there wasn't a huge market of sick people wanting to be spat upon, Bech Chuom lived with his wife and grandchildren while relying on a monthly check of $551 of Supplemental Security Income (SSI) for the elderly. As he expressed to the *New York Times* reporter, he had no means of supporting his family if he were to be cut from benefits. He was too old and weak.

Besides their fear and anxiety over their livelihood, our refugee neighbors were angered that the U.S. government was reneging on its promises. Another neighbor who was interviewed for the *Times* article, Tith Chan, depended on the $707 a month he received in welfare to pay for rent and food for his sick wife and three children. His rent for the Oak Park one-bedroom apartment was $450 a month, so that left only $257 left to pay monthly bills. Although he got some job training and ESL classes, he did not gain enough skills or English proficiency to earn a livable wage. In our low-income neighborhood, job opportunities were limited, especially for those who didn't speak English well. Tith Chan, justifiably embittered, complained, "When we first came here, the Americans said, 'We will help you.' And now they want to change this law. Why?"

Cutting refugees from welfare and food stamps was grossly unjust when one realizes that Southeast Asian refugees fought for the Central Intelligence Agency during the U.S. Secret War in Laos. To interdict traffic on the Ho Chi Minh Trail during the Vietnam War, the U.S. dropped more than two million tons of bombs on Laos. The CIA covertly enlisted Laotian, Hmong, Khmu, and Mien soldiers to fight as their proxy against the Communist Pathet Lao forces. In return, the agency promised that the U.S. government would resettle and care for them as they would U.S. veterans.[7]

When OPMers learned of the welfare reform legislation, we again began to organize the community. Working with a larger coalition of Asian American nonprofit organizations, we sought to inform the public about the disastrous consequences of the law if it were to pass. Oak Park tenants boldly shared their stories in a variety of media outlets, as Bech Chuom and Tith Chan did for the *New York Times*.

> On Mother's Day, Oak Park mothers joined with hundreds of other Asian American mothers in a letter-writing campaign to California's two senators. Kim, one of the mothers in our Oak Park ESL class, was quoted in an editorial by William Wong of the *Oakland Tribune* newspaper. She explained how disappointed she was, as a mother, about not being able to provide for her children: "The kids ask about Christmas gifts. They want a lot of

things, when I can only buy them shoes." Another elderly woman, Lac Diep Tran, complained about Americans'
compassion gap for others and their lack of support
for refugees. She then concluded about the need for
American corporate responsibility, not just personal responsibility: "If the government won't help us, who will?"[8]

In addition to highlighting the injustices of welfare reform, we
lobbied to encourage California state legislators to ameliorate the worst
aspects of the legislation. We argued that poor, noncitizen families
should at least be able to receive food stamps and that the elderly and
disabled needed Social Security. Phannara, wife of Tith Chan, had lost
her entire family during the Killing Fields and continued to suffer from
post-traumatic stress in the form of headaches, dizziness, and sleepless
nights. Twenty years after the genocide, she was in no condition to learn
English well, let alone survive a standard forty-hour work week. Yet she
proudly journeyed to Sacramento with me, on a bus with dozens of other
disabled Asian American mothers, to convince legislators to restore their
meager benefits.

In the meantime, we worked with Oak Park families to obtain citizenship so that they could continue receiving benefits. Our ESL class
shifted to become a citizenship class, and we labored to instruct our
neighbors about the three branches of the American government and
about American history. When we asked who were the first to live in the
United States, our students would respond with their halting, Khmer
accents, "Ne-ga-tive Americans." "No, not ne*ga*tive. Native Americans!"
we would try to correct, but then would add, "But they had the right to
be negative for having their lands taken."

As expected, once welfare reform was implemented, tens of thousands of immigrants applied for citizenship. For Oak Park residents,
the citizenship application process and test compounded the unfairness
of welfare reform. On poverty incomes, they had to pay hundreds of
dollars for fingerprinting and application fees. The wait for their test

appointments was so long that they could lose their benefits before they had a chance to become citizens. Taking the test was traumatizing as well. As in Cambodia, our neighbors had to endure a government interrogation before they were allowed to survive.

By 1997, Oak Park families emerged from welfare reform scathed, but still resilient. Fortunately, many of our neighbors succeeded in becoming naturalized—not just to preserve benefits, but so they could vote and have a say in issues such as welfare and immigration. Bech Chuom and Phannara were able to keep their SSI elderly and disabled benefits. Tith Chan entered a work program at a Ghirardelli chocolate factory.

The United States may have welcomed Southeast Asians as refugees in the 1980s, but by the mid-'90s our nation suffered from compassion fatigue and all sorts of anti-immigrant legislation were being proposed. The experience of living through the Killing Fields in Cambodia is unfathomable for me. Yet for Cambodians who have resettled into America's poor neighborhoods, moving to California was just as traumatizing![9] Acculturative stress—the difficulties of relocating, learning the language, facing violence and racial discrimination, and surviving substandard conditions without work—directly and daily affected my neighbors. Getting cut from their main means of financial support obviously escalated this stress.

In America, the call for personal responsibility is strong. Sadly, the practice of corporate responsibility for our neighbor has been neglected.

Conditions for Change

Refugee agencies resettled families into our neighborhood because it had some of the least expensive rents in the Bay Area. Mien families from Laos and Cambodians first moved to Oak Park in the mid-'80s, the third wave of Southeast Asian refugees to arrive.[10] Once groups became concentrated in Oakland, other refugee families made secondary migrations to our community to join their co-ethnics. Later, Bosnian refugees moved into the apartment complex next to Oak Park in the mid-'90s. In

2014, families from Burma, Bhutan, Syria, Iraq, and Afghanistan also made their home in this neighborhood.

Charging low rents, owners of apartment complexes with refugees have little incentive to repair and maintain their units since they receive small returns on their investment. They also recognize that refugees, who receive some government housing subsidies, will pay their rents and won't know how to go about lodging a complaint. The deterioration of urban slum housing becomes a downward spiral: refugees move in because of cheap rents, and owners do not repair the units. The large family sizes of refugees often bring more wear and tear on the buildings, which then become further dilapidated. For example, black mold spread across the ceilings of Oak Park units because of the dampness. Not only did the roofs leak, but the high number of tenants kept the rooms warm and moist, further spreading mold.

Oak Park had always been derelict, but the rains of El Nino in 1997 exposed how badly the buildings had deteriorated. The sewers and drainage systems backed up so severely that the entire courtyard flooded and threatened to overflow into the bottom-floor apartments. Señora Hortensia Alvarez described vividly how sewage ruined her entire apartment: "Around 1998 all the filth started coming out of the bathroom. The whole hallway, everything was full of water! At that time, I didn't have the money to just go somewhere else to sleep with my kids."

Although the management steam-cleaned the carpeting, the stench remained. Señora Alvarez remembered, "It was worse when it dried. A smell lingered that no one could stomach. It took two days to clean up, but the smell lasted more than a week."

The management also failed to maintain the property properly. Trash littered the courtyard, condoms were left in the parking lot by johns, the complex lacked fire extinguishers, and extermination service was a rarity. Hortensia joked about our situation: "We couldn't stand the cockroaches! Honestly, one went into Mario's ear! He once got sick, and when he came out of the hospital, a cockroach went into his ear. We were almost going to take him right back to the hospital!"

The rains also dripped through the roofing and down the walls. OPM members living at Oak Park suffered through the same conditions. In one apartment, we could see the ceiling literally undulate as swells of water above lapped against the roof. Christine Ma narrowly escaped when a 2-by-4-foot chunk of her ceiling collapsed onto her bed; she fortunately wasn't asleep there at the time. The walls had become so weakened by water rot that when Cameron Cardona leaned against his shower stall to soap his feet, he fell through the wall! When the rains stopped and one boy on a bike accidently bumped a post holding up a stairwell, the entire post fell over. No one was hurt that time, but in another incident, a child fell eight feet to the ground when a stair step collapsed beneath him.

That winter, six children from different Oak Park apartments had to be hospitalized with asthma attacks. Their units were so moist, the mold had spread so far, and the cockroaches left so many droppings that we had an environmental epidemic. Later, when we had children from three different apartments tested, all had mold spores in their bloodstream.

Dan took on the position of resident manager of Oak Park and tried to make repairs to the complex. He quickly learned, however, that the landlords deferred much of the maintenance at the apartments. They did piecemeal, patch-up jobs to the roof and to walls, which soon needed further repairs. The management even tore up asbestos tiles at Oak Park without proper safeguards. Dan observed, "Our building took in $25,000 per month, and I was only given $150 a month for repairs. What I saw in this building was active, calculated neglect—not just passive, benign neglect." He quit after just a few months because he knew he didn't have the funds or support to bring the building to a liveable condition.

In an effort to improve our housing, I enlisted an attorney, Jay Koslofsky, for legal advice. He recommended that we file a lawsuit against our landlords in order to pressure them. Initially, we didn't want any financial damages to be paid or even to take our landlords to court; we just wanted safe housing that was brought up to code and where we wouldn't have to use umbrellas inside our apartments.

Koslofsky also suggested that we would have a stronger case if more tenants, particularly those with egregious damages, signed on to the lawsuit. So OPM members met with each household individually, surveying them about the damages caused by the rain and mold and informing them of their housing rights.

After we surveyed everyone, we held meetings. Since Oak Park families had become accustomed to coming over to our apartment for meetings regarding the police, welfare reform, and housing complaints, having them walk ten yards for another coffee and dessert session seemed natural.

While organizing meetings was easy, gaining support for a lawsuit remained highly unlikely. Most of the Latinos were undocumented, so they feared they might be reported to immigration officials if they complained. The Cambodians had been persecuted by the Khmer Rouge government, and they were very reluctant to deal with any legal process as well. They were doubly fearful they might lose their welfare benefits if they complained too much, even though such fears had no basis. Sophy was one such individual, apprehensive about government or landlord retaliation. "I didn't know my rights or the process of suing. I was living in Oak Park and thought it was wrong to complain," she explained. "I was afraid to join the lawsuit because I didn't really know what would happen, and I was afraid of getting into any controversy because I was on welfare."

Along with the cultural and political barriers, our neighbors had huge economic reasons not to rock the boat. During this period, rents in the neighborhood went as high as $1,200 per month for a one bedroom, while rent at Oak Park was about $450. Given their low, fixed incomes, if the tenants were to lose their housing at Oak Park for some reason, they would not be able to afford continuing to live in Oakland. Alejandra expressed this grave concern: "I was scared at first, thinking they might throw us out on the street. I first thought we shouldn't get involved because they'll kick us out and we'd have to look for another apartment. Other places say you can't have kids, a lot of requirements. They also ask for large deposits, and we couldn't afford such changes."

Our neighbors' precarious financial situations kept them living in fear and in squalid conditions.

Organizing for Change

Even though we came in as outsiders, we OPMers did bring some assets that made us an effective organizing team. Dan had built strong relationships with both Cambodians and Latinos over his eight years at Oak Park, and he got to know everyone while he was resident manager. Not only had I studied Ethnic Studies and social movements, but I had worked on successful political campaigns based on organizing models. Alice Wu and Christina Ma worked with planning and housing organizations that promoted community participation. Carlos Flores, who had worked as a neighborhood community organizer in the past, translated in Spanish. The broader network of Asian American community nonprofit agencies, which also worked with Oak Park tenants, also supported our efforts. For instance, Asian Community Mental Health Services allowed their counselor, Suon In, to interpret in Khmer for us at our tenant meetings.

As we agitated for change, a key event sparked our campaign. In social movements, organizers speak of galvanizing moments that serve as symbolic cues for people to act. When Rosa Parks refused to move to the back of the bus, for example, she signaled that African Americans were not going to stand for segregation. We had a similar incident and similarly courageous individuals at Oak Park.

Perhaps unaware that we were organizing to sue, the landlords announced a badly timed rent increase, which infuriated the tenants. The notification of the rent hike represented the greediness and negligence of our landlords. They had lost the tenants' respect and their legitimacy as landlords deserving our regular rent checks.

Then, when the representative of the management company came for yet another meeting, grandmother Touch Phan erupted in anger. Arguing in Khmer, she complained, "We have rodents everywhere, there's mold in the walls, and the ceiling is leaking. We're angry because the landlord doesn't care and nothing's being fixed!" The representative stepped back, stunned at the ferocity of this small Asian matriarch. She was our Rosa Parks, a community leader who stood to confront our injustices.

Dan later laughed, "Touch Phan opened Pandora's box!" Once this elder in the community vocalized her grievances, others joined in to express their housing issues. The grandmas seemed to start a game of one-upmanship, in which Khlot Ry tried to show her apartment was worse than Touch Phan's. "You say you have leaks?!? I have a typhoon surging through my room . . .," she seemed to complain. I wouldn't know exactly, because I just heard a lot of incomprehensible yelling in Khmer that the translator couldn't keep up with.

And so, the fight was on, and our neighbors began to stand up for themselves collectively.

Bringing together everyone in our cramped living room brought the two ethnic groups closer. In these sessions, Kosal Kong recognized that we all shared the same material conditions. He commented, "We are all people in the same situation going through the same things, and we just need to help each other and work together. It doesn't matter to me what race someone is, as long as we are together and are working together."

Amongst themselves in smaller groups, Oak Park tenants would discuss the information and results of these meetings and decide among themselves whether to join the lawsuit. Both ethnic communities at Oak Park included extended families in different units. One couple, Felix and Hortensia, vocally supported the lawsuit and facilitated organizing through their relationships. Felix developed friendships with other Spanish-speaking men at Oak Park and assisted them in getting work. Hortensia would cook and sell tamales together with her next-door neighbor. These personal ties provided the trust necessary to work together.

Most adults agreed to the lawsuit because they learned about their housing rights and what legal protections they had from eviction. They made decisions based on rational choices and probabilities. Alejandra recognized, "We were all going through the same issues together, and we knew we had rights." Another tenant, Juan, realized that he had nothing to lose: "Daniel told me that there was an option. If we win, good. If we don't, we don't. We weren't sure if we were going to win or not. I saw that everyone else was joining. So I told Daniel, 'Just put us down. We're with you . . . whatever happens, happens.'"

Oak Park members also traded the respect which we had earned for a hearing among our neighbors. Kosal explained, "When Russell and everyone talked with us, told us the process, and gave us all the information, we decided to join the lawsuit. I thought it was a good idea. Since Russell and everyone was helping with it, we felt they knew what they were doing and felt confident. We weren't afraid."

The elders, though, went along with the group decision mostly in order to support us and the overall community. Khlot Ry didn't even want to participate in the legal action. She actually felt sorry for the landlords, explaining, "What would they eat if they lose their house?" Yet once she saw others sign on, she bowed to community pressure as well.

When we filed our lawsuit, 44 of the 56 households at Oak Park were listed. In total, we had 197 plaintiffs in our case, almost all of whom were noncitizen, limited-English-speaking, and low-income immigrants. That was the major victory in our organizing—not that we would win a lawsuit or obtain decent housing, but that our community rallied together to improve our situation.

The *Oakland Tribune* newspaper announced our lawsuit with the headline, "Shabby Building Spurs Formation of Unlikely Tenants Association."[11] We were unlikely combatants coming together in a housing struggle: undocumented Latinos, Cambodian refugees, and evangelical college grads. Carlos shared our approach of mobilizing our neighbors: "People have a desire to make things better for themselves, to make things that are unjust, just. But a lot of times, people don't know how to do so even though they see something is really wrong. Organizing brings a broader perspective of the wider systemic injustices. God really wants justice to happen, so organizing people for justice on earth brings hope to people and a wider perspective. And that's related to my faith in the gospel."

Here, God's miracle was that he saw Carlos's faith and brought hope to us. He drew us together to overcome our language barriers that kept us from developing trust. He reconciled our ethnic differences that made us suspicious. He surmounted our political fears to give us hope and a wider perspective. Through the leadership of our elders, who weren't only thinking of themselves but of the entire community, God spurred us to take a united stand. Amazingly, he used a shabby building to form a community in the likeness of his kingdom.

Interceding for Change

Once the city issued fines for housing violations and we initiated our lawsuit, the landlords did not repair the buildings as we expected. Instead, our landlords claimed corporate bankruptcy just two months after our filing and let the complex fall into greater disrepair. They apparently tried to delay court hearings and outlast the tenants, who began to move away because of the dilapidating conditions. The neighborhood was suffering "blight"—deterioration of buildings, facilities, and land use detrimental to the health and safety of the community.

We had used up all the organizing tactics we had in our bag. We had already made use of our political connections and had requested our city councilmember, Ignacio De La Fuente, to initiate the housing inspections of our site. Our lawsuit even spurred a local initiative coordinated by De La Fuente's aide, Libby Schaaf, to educate other immigrant communities about their housing rights.[12] So many plaintiffs joined the case that our attorney secured the services of a leading San Francisco law firm specializing in tenant issues. We sought as much media attention as we could, using the angle of our multiethnic coalition to draw press. Oak Park became the symbol of Oakland's worst slum. When Councilmember De La Fuente's Decent Housing Task Force named the city's seven worst apartment complexes, it hosted its press conference at our complex.[13] Despite these legal, political, and media efforts, our landlord's bankruptcy put the status of Oak Park in limbo.

Like the children of Israel and the Hakka, we seemed destined to move from secure homes to wandering in the wilderness.

Since the building was condemned, vacant units were boarded up so that Oak Park looked increasingly like an abandoned lot of buildings. Carlos recounted the low point of our housing struggle: "This time during the lawsuit was very distressing, that we let down all the people. It was really scary, the possibility that people would be displaced and the community would break up." As much as we wanted to change our housing conditions, we were far more concerned that our friends and family be able to stay together.

At the end of our rope, we began to pray even more earnestly and regularly than before at OPM meetings. We found ourselves praying as Nehemiah did when he wept over the ruins of Jerusalem and the remnant left there (Neh. 1:15–11). First, we confessed our sins and prayed for ourselves by praying for our landlords. Secular communities often build unity among its members by vilifying the enemy. We at Oak Park saw our landlords as callous to our plight, especially when we thought of the sick elderly and children at the apartment. Yet we were reminded to love our enemies and to forgive them. Indeed, we wanted God's love to motivate us, not cold anger and bitterness.

Second, we lifted up our neighbors and lamented alongside them. They didn't have the options to move homes as easily as the OPM members. We grieved over the politics and policies that brought them to the United States, from the civil war that caused Cambodians to flee, to the grinding poverty in Mexico that offered no opportunities. One time, as we considered the inhospitable welcome that our neighbors received—including being denied welfare and profiled as criminals—the group of us broke down, weeping uncontrollably. Our longing was succinctly summarized in the Lord's prayer, "Your kingdom come, your will be done, on earth as it is in heaven" (Matt. 6:10).

At one point, when I despaired about the depth of sin and injustice in Oakland, I felt justified in seriously questioning where God was. Upon listening to my grievances, a wise Maryknoll nun gently replied to me,

"Of course God is in Oakland. Jesus is at Oak Park, because you are there. Jesus is in you."

Jesus is present, in me and through me. This profound mystery of God's incarnation never fails to amaze me. Though I don't think I'll ever grasp the enormity of this truth, it did spur me to continue his work and to love my neighbors.

Third, we prayed for success and favor within the legal system and the powers that be. We hoped that by shining a light in the darkness, God would drive out evil through the authorities he had appointed on earth.

Through our repentance of our self-righteous anger and lamentation over the nation's policies, by our intercession for our neighborhood and our supplication for favor in the eyes of the government, we prayed for the peace of our community, so that we too might have peace.

Changes for Oak Park

Our lawsuit was at an impasse for a year while the landlord's case remained in bankruptcy court. In the meantime, Oak Park went under federal receivership, since the owners owed money to Fannie Mae, the government association that had provided the mortgage loans. Minor improvements were made but no new tenants could move in. The building was still considered uninhabitable by the city and its vacant units remained boarded.

A few weeks after we visited the heebie-jeebies *Psycho* apartment for a possible mass relocation, we finally received a breakthrough. Our attorneys informed us that our landlords made no appearance at bankruptcy court. So working with a Deputy City Attorney, aptly named Johnny Angel, our tenants association came up with our own bankruptcy plan for Oak Park Apartments. Oak Park's three main creditors—Fannie Mae, the City of Oakland, and the Tenants Association—each had their own financial interests to claim from the landlords. Nevertheless, we formed another unlikely group to develop a joint plan to take over Oak Park.

About to lose their investment, our landlords came to settle. The tenants agreed to end our dispute only on the condition that Oak Park be brought up to code, put on the market, and made permanent affordable housing. We even found two nonprofit developers, the East Bay Asian Local Development Corporation (EBALDC) and Affordable Housing Associates (AHA), who were willing to purchase our complex. In the past, Carlos and Alice had worked for EBALDC and Christine had been staff at AHA, so our connections once again came in handy. The City of Oakland agreed to provide these developers funding to buy Oak Park, so our landlords didn't really lose; they still earned a profit from their investment.

Finally, three years after our initial organizing efforts, the Oak Park Tenants Association achieved our housing victory. Oak Park was sold and came under the management of award-winning, nonprofit developers. We received $950,000 in damages; each household got a small amount, and the bulk of the remaining funds went to families whose children suffered severe injuries or illnesses from their apartments' poor conditions.

I have never had a dramatic born-again testimony where God saved me from some debilitating addiction or incurable disease. Instead, the Oak Park victories are my testaments to God's power to redeem. Both my neighbors taking a stand and the housing settlement where everyone won were miraculous. God answered our prayers, and like Nehemiah, we found favor in the sight of government to rebuild Oak Park's walls.

After Nehemiah rebuilt Jerusalem's walls and people returned to the city, they gathered in the town square by the water gate. To the assembled body, Nehemiah declared, "Go and enjoy choice food and sweet drinks, and send some to those who have nothing prepared. This day is holy to our Lord. Do not grieve, for the joy of the LORD is your strength" (Neh. 8:10). They celebrated with thanksgiving by eating and by remembering the poor.

On that Thanksgiving in 2000, we did the same thing. Oak Park tenants, along with Councilmember De La Fuente, representatives from EBALDC and AHA, and our attorneys and translators, partied one more time in the courtyard of Oak Park. Like Nehemiah and the assembled exiles, we rejoiced. Our community had been reclaimed.

Unintended Changes

After the legal victory, OPM members moved out, since most of us married and resettled in the neighborhood. Joan Kim married me in 2002, and she got a taste of living at Oak Park before the new complex was built. When she returned home from medical school, bunches of children would scream and hug her on her way to the door. We would order noodles from the apartment above, and bowls of soup would be hand delivered, complete with lime slices and basil.

One morning, as she ate cereal, Joan spied a cockroach on our window blind. Remembering my stories of when I first moved in with Dan a decade prior, she took out a lighter and sought to firebomb the roach. Unfortunately, she couldn't ignite the lighter quickly enough. When she finally got the flame torch to work, the roach and blinds were so doused with Lysol that they were instantaneously torched. When I came home later that day and saw our melted blinds, I nodded my head and thought, "Just another day at Oak Park."

By the fall of 2002, Oak Park had been reconstructed and our neighbors moved into their rehabbed apartments. Kosal's family of seven went from a one-bedroom shared with mice to a sparkling four-bedroom apartment with new appliances and ambient floor heating. That year, a brand new school campus had been built in our neighborhood, so Felix and Hortensia's five children got spanking new classrooms as well as a new home. Veasina, now with a room where she could study, enthused, "We never thought we could have it so good." Asthma attacks declined precipitously just from the change of the housing conditions.

With the new property management and the reconstructed apartments, the tenants took much better care of their environment. When Dan was apartment manager, I would help him sweep up the courtyard and I'd collect canfuls of litter. Dozens of beer bottle caps would get embedded in the dirt patches where grass once grew. Now, Oak Park remained pristine. Even the ice cream cart vendors would make sure that kids no longer threw their wrappers on the ground.

OPM members took our lawsuit winnings and bought the house in front of Oak Park, situated between its two parking lots. Vacant and abandoned, it had once been used by heroin addicts as a shooting gallery. Later, a large Oak Park family rented the unit. With generous, additional funding from Berkeley Covenant Church, we were able to add another floor to the building so that this family could remain in the neighborhood. On the first floor, we established Little Sprouts Preschool for the community.

These positive environmental changes, though, had some unintended consequences. Oak Park's courtyard, once bustling with kids playing and adults gambling, quieted down. Neighborly social interactions declined as families spent more time indoors. After children got their own bedrooms, they preferred to stay inside, playing video games or studying.

Oak Park families won the American dream and obtained housing that met federal standards. Accordingly, they adopted American suburban lifestyles: privatized and nuclear-family centered. As their children got older, they were also less likely to go outside and play all day.

Unfortunately, Joan and I had to finally move out because we earned too much to live in a subsidized complex. Although we and other OPM members chose to remain in the neighborhood, our contact with Oak Park tenants became less frequent as we started our own family lives.

One other factor made Oak Park more sterile. Other youth used to come visit Oak Park because of its lively atmosphere. However, some of them began to gamble, deal drugs, and argue with neighbors. They would also hang out in front of Little Sprouts Preschool and occasionally get into fights with other gangs. Neighbors began to complain about them, and the local neighborhood crime prevention council took up Oak Park as one of its targeted spots to clean up. The City of Oakland even warned us that Little Sprouts and EBALDC would receive fines if we didn't install fencing and keep the youth away. Ironically, the blight law used against us had been established by the Decent Housing Task Force—the same legislation initially created to help Oak Park!

With newly installed fencing, security gates, and more lighting, Oak Park became like a prison for the youth. Some Oak Park families were even evicted because their youth caused so much trouble. These stringent measures, along with the heightened surveillance, made Oak Park more quiet and peaceful, but less welcoming and lively.

Whenever I get together with Oak Park youth, we fondly recall the old days of pandemonium and rue the new Oak Park. Our story of community organizing for justice didn't necessarily have a happily-ever-after ending. We obtained justice, but lost a bit of community.

Epilogue

The Oak Park housing lawsuit is bittersweet to me. When Oak Park was rebuilt and tenants moved into their new homes, it seemed like we had a happy ending, where God's goodness and justice had prevailed. Today, a decade later, I feel like I've lost the community that gave me so much joy, meaning, and friendship. I once gain feel like a Hakka, in exile from home and community. Was justice won?

This question haunts me. As an American Christian, I expect—and even feel entitled to—justice and happy endings. Some of us are optimistic and hopeful that we can effect social change. Christians who aim for the flourishing of our cities suggest that we use our power and privilege to transform communities. As Andy Crouch writes, "The institutions of our time will be changed not by impersonal institutional forces; they will be changed by trustees, the image bearers who face their institutions' failings, forgive them and lead toward a better way."[14] We at OPM tried to use all the resources at our disposal—including our political connections, media strategies, and legal institutions—to renew our neighborhood. We earnestly prayed to be an effective witness of God's good news. And yet, our efforts could be seen as less than completely successful.

Other Christians are much less sanguine, and argue that we should not have expected to transform the world. Instead, they believe we can only seek to be faithful, countercultural colonies who present prophetic challenges to the world's powers that be, as Stanley Hauerwas advises: "We argue that the political task of the church is to be the church rather than to transform the world."[15] If that is so, then I could easily lapse into apathy about broad, societal concerns, since the church seems so irrelevant and I can only impact a small few.

Between these two extreme American Christian responses—that we should aim to be triumphal and powerful or we should merely seek to be faithful and countercultural—the prophet Jeremiah and my refugee neighbors have offered me a balanced, Asian-exilic perspective on justice. Their insights about seeking shalom while in exile are especially pertinent for the American church today, as it declines in cultural influence, political power, and sheer numbers.

As they longed for shalom and rest, Jeremiah's letter to the exiles instructs them how they should live in a foreign, hostile land:

> Build houses and settle down; plant gardens and eat what they produce. Marry and have sons and daughters; find wives for your sons and give your daughters in marriage, so that they too may have sons and daughters. Increase in number there; do not decrease. Also, seek the peace and prosperity of the city to which I have carried you into exile. Pray to the Lord for it, because if it prospers, you too will prosper (Jer. 29:5–7).

Jeremiah's instructions are surprising, because the exiles longed to return to their homeland, where they could better control their destinies. Instead, the prophet said to seek the prosperity of their enemies—in the very place of their desolation and trauma.

First, Jeremiah informs us to invest in the places of our exile. Settling down is a way of doing justice and seeking peace because it requires an investment in relationships. Bech Chuom, the Khmer native healer, exemplified how God's shalom involves a relational practice of right relations with others.

When almost two hundred of my neighbors joined the lawsuit against our landlord, most of the younger people did so in order to protect their rights. Some of the others signed on because they trusted the leadership of the tenants association. Bech Chuom, however, gave an unusual reason to participate. "I joined the lawsuit because I felt sorry for you!" he told me through a translator. "I saw you knocking on everyone's doors, so then I wanted to help you."

This grandfather saw that we Christians had been acting as a family by taking corporate responsibility for the entire community. He simply wanted to reciprocate and support me, because I was like his family.

Settling down, building family ties, and taking on mutual responsibility for one another is the first step in doing God's justice. Righteousness, and then peace, emerge when we are rooted and invested in each other's lives and take responsibility for each other. In the United States, we tend to believe that justice is an individual right that we need to defend. For Bech Chuom, justice required assuming one's corporate responsibility: we are obligated to take care of one another, and reciprocate the care that we have received. In this sense, injustice occurs when we do not take care of one another, whether on an individual or systemic level.

When we take care of each other as family, then God's shalom is present.

Second, Jeremiah calls on the exiles to seek and work for the shalom of the city. This shalom—the peace and prosperity—takes an active participation and commitment. As I stated, our lowest point in our three-year lawsuit was when Oak Park was condemned as uninhabitable. When I asked him how he felt at the time we thought we would lose our homes, Bech Chuom just joked, "I didn't worry. I would just go move into a big home with you!" In the face of oppression and immigrant exploitation, he took a step of faith and trust to simply join with his community.

I would argue that doing justice as powerless exiles is like this—it's an act of trust and obedience to God's commands. We do not know if we will be successful in winning justice; after all, those Jewish exiles would never see their homeland again. At the same time, we do not have to be resigned to being ineffective and weak in this fallen world.

As Isaiah described God's kingdom of justice, "The fruit of that righteousness will be peace; its effect will be quietness and confidence forever" (Isa. 32:17–18). Similarly, Jesus promised that if we abide and remain in his love, we will bear much fruit, whether that fruit is love, new members in his kingdom, or justice. We need to have a trust and compliance like Bech Chuom in order to follow God's will for shalom. We merely work for peace by having right relations, and it is up to God to bear the fruit.

This hope for God's fruit of peace encourages us to work for justice, while freeing us from the need to save the world. In doing justice, I don't hope to be successful. I am not resigned to just being faithful. I aim to abide in Jesus, and to be fruitful.

Lastly, Jeremiah calls on the exiles to pray for the city of Babylon. Prayer itself is an act of peace and justice. While Americans often think that justice needs to be achieved with power and activism, exiles know of their true citizenship and acknowledge the primary source of change.

What could be more justice-seeking than to plead for mercy before God, whom James calls the only "Lawgiver and Judge" (James 4:12)? Like the persistent widow who goes to the judge's door at night for bread, we must go to our good Father, who will grant us good things. Jesus himself taught us to pray daily, "your kingdom come, your will be done, on earth as it is in heaven" (Matt. 6:10).

On more than one occasion, my great-grandmother had to go to court in order to protect her livelihood, as well as her home. We at Oak Park also had to argue our case before judges to gain a settlement. At the end, we were at the mercy of our heavenly Judge.

Prayers made for peace and prosperity are similar; the cries of the oppressed and exploited are our pleas before the high court of heaven. Our only hope for shalom is from God.

As exiles, we American Christians need to recognize how we are foreigners and strangers in this world, as the author of Hebrew exhorts.[16] While looking for a better country of our own, we must act like Hall Gock Tie, my Hakka great-grandmother, and Bech Chuom, my refugee neighbor. We must act like family to one another in taking corporate responsibility for the greater good. And ultimately, we must seek the favor of the High Judge of Heaven and pray like the psalmist: "Awake, my God; decree justice!" (Psalm 7:6).

CHAPTER 5

Tiger Moms, Teddy Bear Dads, and a Panda Father

The day before we met the girls in April 2011, Joan and I were scared to death. It felt as if we were entering an arranged marriage. We were going to be bonded to these strangers for life, but Bethsy and Bonny could be axe murderers, for all we knew.

About a year earlier, I had seen a poster on a BART subway car. Below a picture of a doe-eyed, plaintive-looking youth, the billboard called out to me: "Change a life. Foster a refugee child."

"We could do that!" I told myself a bit brashly. I had spent eighteen years living with Cambodian and Mien families who resettled to our neighborhood. And Joan and I had conducted an extensive needs-assessment of refugees from Burma that had shaped local policy. As a pediatrician at a neighborhood health clinic, Joan had probably cared for more refugee youth than any other doctor in the area. If anybody was prepared to change a life and foster a refugee child, we were.

But the decision to become foster parents to Bethsy and Bonny had to be made quickly, so we hadn't had much time to consider its enormity. We had a flurry of things to do in order to ready our home. Foster care families, by law, must have fire extinguishers ready, household poisons put away, and even knives stored in locked cabinets.

Just before the girls arrived, I realized that I had no actual clue about how to raise daughters, let alone teenage ones. Our own son, Matthew, was just six years old at the time, and any dysfunctions we had inflicted upon him had yet to appear. So as naive parents, Joan and I rushed to the local Barnes & Noble bookstore and scanned all the books on parenting teenagers. We eventually bought *You and Your Adolescent: The Essential Guide for Ages 10–25*.[1]

This book only raised more fears and anxieties as we hastily made up a list of ground rules for the girls. Despite our united front in parental discipline, the two of us could not foresee how our family might change. We didn't know if these girls cut classes, if they dated guys with tongue piercings, or if they, in the worst-case scenario, didn't take off their shoes upon entering a home and left stains on my precious carpet.

We couldn't just return them because of customer dissatisfaction, even if we did have a receipt. They were coming to be part of our family. For Asian Americans, that means almost everything.

The Fears and Horrors of Tiger Parenting

Since family is so valued, Joan and I prepared for parenthood like any good Asian American: we studied the best books on how to raise strong families. Two models—Tiger moms and Teddy Bear dads—had great ideas, but each approached being family in very different ways.

In 2011, the *Wall Street Journal* printed a somewhat controversial headline. It read, "Why Chinese Mothers Are Superior." To me, the headline was just common sense—of course Chinese mothers are superior. Just look at all the Chinese people in the world! Who else produces so many children? And with a one-child policy, at that.

That essay—excerpted portions of Amy Chua's book *Battle Hymn of the Tiger Mother*—explained why Chinese "Tiger Moms" raise such stereotypically successful children. They just demand perfection in return for the extreme sacrifice that immigrant parents make. Now that I think of it, God expects the same.[2]

As an Asian American, I can appreciate Tiger parenting. So much so that I married a cub of a Tiger mom. My partner, Joan, is a prototypical Asian American model minority who was raised with a strong Asian upbringing. Her Korean immigrant parents purposely moved into neighborhoods with the best public schools. Although she didn't speak English when she entered kindergarten, she eventually became class valedictorian in one of California's top high schools and scored almost perfect on her SATs. Despite that setback on the SATs, she continued to work hard. She practiced concert piano up to three hours a day when she competed on a national level.

Young Joan taught Sunday school at her home church and volunteered at a homeless shelter on her own while just a junior in high school. Obviously, she got into every elite university to which she applied and she graduated from Harvard. She would have found a cure for attention deficit hyperactivity disorder, but she was too busy training for the heptathlon in the 1992 Summer Olympics at Barcelona. Okay, I made up the last sentence, but the rest is true about her work ethic and attainments.

Although Joan accomplished much as a result of her parents' child-rearing, utilizing the Tiger mom method doesn't necessarily lead to successful children. Not everyone can be a Joan, and seeking to emulate her would probably lead to never-ending frustration and perpetual self-doubt. At least, that's what has happened to me.

What's forgotten in the making of these whiz kids is that Amy Chua's daughters and Joan come from parents who are themselves high-achieving. Asian Americans arrive to the United States through a process of selective immigration, in which the United States prioritizes professionals for admission. Our nation receives the best and brightest from Asian countries such as China, South Korea, and India. These parents, then, are able to offer their second-generation children the advantages of excellent schools, close and careful parental supervision, and bountiful extracurricular resources. Without minimizing the hard work of Chua's daughters or Joan, their accomplishments can be seen as a privilege of class and race.

The popular cultural stereotype is that Asian Americans are the model minority because of their hard work, value for education, and respect for authority. Beneath this begrudging respect, though, is a fear and resentment that Asian Americans, as the "Yellow Horde," may be taking over.[3]

One response of sour grapes, often made to Amy Chua and even posted in the *New York Times*, is that white American parenting remains better than Asian Tiger parenting. Although Asian students may score higher on tests, white youth are said to be more socially competent with "enhanced emotional functioning." In comparison to Chinese and Chinese American parents, it seems that white parents tend to be irrationally supportive, so that their kids turn out more well-rounded and, eventually, happy.

That's how I respond to Joan's achievements. Even at our wedding rehearsal party, person after person joked about how I was bound to lose every argument to her because she's so much smarter than I am. Well, she may be highly accomplished, brilliant, and cultured, but at least I'm well-rounded! I've become nicely plump, as my father taught me to enjoy the football 49ers, baseball Giants, and basketball Warriors from my couch.

The Ethnocentric American Teddy Bear Family

Instead of Tiger parenting, the American mainstream model of family is the teddy bear, which is great for hugs and cuddles. American evangelicals often adopt this model and identify the Teddy Bear family as the prescribed, universal, and biblical way to be.[4]

In the United States, marriages are supposed to be partnerships of romantic love and intimacy, where we take long walks on the beach, read poetry to one another, and dance into the sunset. Ever expressive, we are to communicate in one of the five universal love languages, such as gifts of roses or acts of service.[5]

In marriage, we are to dare to love, according to the writers of the best-selling *Love Dare*, a Christian nonfiction book.[6] Like other evangelical books, *The Love Dare* emphasizes that love is an active choice; we need to lead our hearts instead of following our hearts. As spouses dare to love selflessly, then a good marriage promises almost everything: "to eliminate loneliness, multiply our effectiveness, establish family, raise children, enjoy life, and bless us with relational intimacy."[7]

Just as marriage is imagined to be a place of intimacy, families are to be privatized, safe refuges from the dangerous, competitive world outside. Children are to receive nurture and support so that they develop healthy self-concepts and can flourish to their full potential. As they develop, these children differentiate so that they have their own, strong sense of self. If one has healthy boundaries, then one takes ownership and responsibility over one's life.[8]

Another Christian best-seller for over twenty years, *Parenting with Love and Logic*, aims to instill these proper boundaries in children by teaching them to think about and live with their decisions.[9] The authors declare they can restore the fun of parenting and, at the same time, help parents to raise children to become independent problem-solvers: "In short, [*Parenting with Love and Logic*] will teach them responsibility, and that's what parenting is all about."[10]

Parents inculcate this autonomy as they act as advisors, or in the authors' words, "consultants," to their kids. In this role, parents build up a child's self-esteem and confidence in his skills by assisting him in recognizing his own accomplishments. For example, when little Jimmy goes to the potty on his own, a parent should not praise directly but encourage and question. As Matthew's parental consultant, I should say something like, "How do you feel about your risk-taking approach to going poo-poo?" The authors are careful to remind parents that "It is essential to keep the atmosphere around toilet training fun and exciting—even glee-ful."[11] That last imperative sure makes me feel like a failed parent. I never even felt giddy, much less gleeful, during toilet training.

American Teddy Bear families aren't necessarily working, however. Evangelical couples need to start becoming more multilingual in their love languages, because their divorce rate is the same as other Americans at about 42 percent.[12]

Furthermore, our children don't seem to be developing strong boundaries or reaching their potential in becoming responsible for themselves. Over one-third of America's boomerang generation return as adults to live with their parents.[13] Evidently, these adult children have low self-esteem, so they haven't fully individuated. Pitifully, they end up living with their parents who have poor boundaries and just can't say no to their children. Rather than being consultants to their children, they are—to put it frankly—enablers of codependency.

Neither Tiger parenting nor Teddy Bear families seem to fully fit me, either. Admittedly, I am more like a billy goat, gruff and bleating in my familial relations. I propose that another animal, the panda, may offer an alternative model for family life. The Panda family doesn't emphasize strictness and success as the Tiger mom approach does and neither does it stress relational intimacy and individual boundaries the way Teddy Bear families do. Instead, it utilizes Chinese family values to inculcate Christian virtues of faithfulness, community, and interdependence. Such ethics are applicable to all, not just Chinese. After all, pandas are multiracial: they are black, white, and Asian.

My own relationship with Joan models this Panda faithfulness, as she has stuck with me despite my unbearability. (That was not a pun. Pandas aren't bears.) Indeed, my marriage to her isn't based on expressive love or willful choice, but on a deep loyalty by which we trust one another.

The Courtship of St. Joan: The Asian Love Language of Faithful Loyalty

In 1999, I had just returned from running around Oakland's Lake Merritt and was dragging rags around our living room with my feet. That's how I mopped our floor at Oak Park. Usually, Asians take off their shoes upon entering a home, but so many kids came into our apartment that it was too much of a bother. Besides, sometimes they came in already barefoot, so they didn't have any shoes to take off. Consequently, our living room floor was often dusty and filthy, and I had to perform a weekly skating-on-rags routine, very similar to *Disney on Ice*, throughout our home.

Someone rapped on our front door. I wearily opened it, expecting yet another child to run in and mess up my just-cleaned floor. Instead, I opened the door to a magical scene as if *The Lord of the Rings* had been set in East Oakland. In front of me, I gazed upon an elfin creature—if you can picture a Korean American female elf—with the sweetest, most delicate heart-shaped face. She stood there, shifting her glances awkwardly up and down, with her hands in the front pockets of her green linen dress. Dazed for a moment, I was jarred from my reverie by the booming baritone voice of a dwarf-like man standing to the side. "Russell, I'd like you to meet Joan," thundered the short, stout, and bearded Rich Webber, the volunteer coordinator of Harbor House. "She's going to spend the summer with us at Harbor House and I wanted to show her Oak Park. She's getting her degree in public health."

I don't recall much else from this introduction and our quick tour of Oak Park, beyond the fleeting thought that we both wore green linen clothes. Like elves do.

Joan, though, had a more dramatic message that day as she left Oak Park with Rich. I now say it was a message from God, but she might say it was a foreboding threat from the Mouth of Sauron, aka the Voice of the Dread Abomination from *The Lord of the Rings*. In her head, she heard, "You just met the man you're going to marry!"

After the Oak Park community met Joan, members gathered and formed the Fellowship of the Ring. They recognized that I had been a bachelor far too long, and the fellowship initiated a collective quest to convince Joan to marry me. Such a venture was quite perilous, and many hearts had already been broken in vain attempts to secure such a ring. Nonetheless, the fellowship was resolute, and we began our journey to pursue the ring.

Joan and I soon found ourselves invited to the same outings by friends, and we slowly got to know one another. I began to speak of her as St. Joan because of her selfless heart in giving to the poor. Boosted by the valiant efforts of my supporters, including Grandma Ry and the Oak Park children, I sought to woo her. Unfortunately, Joan eventually saw the real me.

My problem, and the reason that it took me four decades before getting married, is that I'm linguistically challenged. Even though I went to Chinese school for years and lived in China and Taiwan for extended periods, I can't speak Chinese. All I've learned to do with my ancestral tongue is to speak English with Cantonese tones. It's a halting, abrupt manner that sounds as if I'm haggling over the price of a skinny chicken at a loud marketplace, even though I may be reciting a love poem to Joan on a solitary walk along a moonlit beach.

Speaking a love language is even more difficult for me. Because of my judgmental and severe orientation, I can be critical and demanding. I don't extend patience or display meekness, but the high expectations of a stern father.

Early on when we were dating, Joan and I drove out to Point Reyes National Seashore for a hike. Despite the picturesque setting, we didn't swoon over each other's company. Instead, we got into one of those silly arguments that escalate quickly. I don't remember the exact issue, but it was probably something as serious as how to shuffle a deck of cards. She employs the overhand shuffle by lifting cards out and replacing them in a different spot; I recommend the riffle shuffle, which in my opinion more elegantly and efficiently randomizes the cards.

Joan would hear my suggestions as critiques, probably because I speak in a halting, abrupt manner that sounds as if I'm shouting at a marketplace. Or perhaps she heard my recommendations as critiques because I'm critical.

I, on the other hand, would complain that Joan's resistance to my wisdom made me feel unheard. As the youngest child in my family, I never had a say in anything and subsequently, I never feel heard. To get heard, I feel the need to speak in increasingly loud, strident tones. Joan, the perfect child who was unaccustomed to being shamed or seen as flawed, then withdrew more.

How to shuffle cards—or any other tiny issue—became entrenched battles between Joan and me over her being accepted and me being heard. Having no boundaries, I would raise my voice in frustration. With intensely personal boundaries, Joan would close herself off. We drove home from Pt. Reyes in smoldering silence, and Joan questioned whether she could remain in a relationship with me.

Even though I tried to employ Joan's language of love—empathetic listening—I could not love as I should. I daily chose to accept her and care for her, yet I failed miserably as I constantly pointed out ways she could change. Tragically, I love badly the person whom I love the most. God is love and I claim to follow him, but I don't seem to have the capacity to love.

What kept us going in our relationship were our Asian background and our Christian hope. As a group, Asians may not always be emotionally intimate or daringly loving in their marriages, but they tend to value loyalty and faithfulness. Loyalty, one of the main virtues of Confucianism, is understood by Asians as the devotion of the soul. It's prized and practiced toward one's nation, one's family, and even one's gang. In the United States, movie heroes are rugged, lonesome cowboys or vigilantes who individually beat the system. In Chinese kung fu movies, however, the hero is the one who sacrifices himself to avenge the honor of his Shaolin temple. Even if the hero dies, he is loyal to the end.

This kind of sacrificial loyalty is best exhibited by God's *hesed*, roughly defined as loving-kindness, to Israel and to his bride, the Church. Despite the continual infidelity of his people, God remains faithful in his actions and loyal to his covenant. Joan's loyalty and *hesed* to me similarly bless me. Even though I screw up time and time again, in my abrupt and halting manner, she remains devoted and constant. Her loving-kindness is something I can count on no matter how unheard I may feel. Likewise, she knows that I will always be present for her, even if I don't seem to accept her fully.

That abiding loyalty, that assumption to always be there for the other, kept us in our relationship. On our engagement day, I led Joan on a treasure hunt in Marin County. Each clue led to a treasure that represented something I cherished about Joan or something I valued highly and wanted to share with her. One clue took us to my beloved Muir Woods, where I roamed as a youth among towering redwoods and learned to wander freely in the glory of creation. There I had the park rangers wear "May I help you, Joan?" badges and let us in for free. The next clue took us to Stinson Beach, where X marked the spot of a buried treasure. Joan dug up a tray of Korean kimbab, rice rolled in seaweed, and a note in which I pledged to honor her family and her background.

Another clue led us back to Point Reyes, the site where we both had been traumatized by that horrible fight. The treasures to be found there were repentance, forgiveness, and redemption. I apologized for our fight on that date and pledged again to seek change. I also asked that our bitter memory of that place be replaced with an even deeper image, that God could heal the scarred places of our hearts and that I could change. Because of Joan's devotion to me, she forgave me and trusted me despite the hurt.

The last clue led us to an overlook at Muir Beach. I had planned to have some friends set up a small table and chairs where we could enjoy Joan's favorite dessert, tiramisu, and watch the sunset. Then I would get on my knee and ask her to be my bride. However, when my friends arrived, they found that another couple had reserved that spot for their wedding!

Since marriage trumps engagement, they couldn't ask that couple to leave.

When Joan and I arrived, though, the wedding party had left. Fortunately, they just had a secular wedding that didn't have much ceremony. After a glorious day in the Marin headlands, Joan said yes to me.

In her words, she said yes because "I could see God's work and promise in Russell. In him I found a partner in following Jesus and in living among those marginalized by the world. God was working in him, despite his flaws, to make him righteous and blameless in his sight. So I was convicted to let go of my misgivings and focus on the reality of Christ's presence in him."

With such forgiveness, faith in God's work in us, and loyalty, Joan and I have partnered to do what we could not have done alone. We explored missions together in far-flung sites, and we remained steadfast in our ministry through some very dark places. We challenged one another to pursue vocations that would be daunting without support. And over time, our fights have decreased in frequency and tenor. I'm learning that I must accept Joan as she is and Joan is taking the time to hear me fully. I still have a long way to go to become fluent in a love language, but at least I have Joan as a conversation partner.

Most of all, in this partnership we have become more open to each other and to others. With a foundation of loyal love, we are able to extend outward. Just as God constantly gathers more to join his church family into one body, Joan and I have been blessed in building our own family.

Living in Oakland, though, raises two issues in bringing up a family. Can they be safe from violence, and will they receive a good education?

Bear Precautions: From Personal Safety to Community Peace

After the Oak Park lawsuit, Dan became pastor of New Hope Covenant Church, an Evangelical Covenant church started by some OPM members and folks from Harbor House. Joan and I joined when we started dating in spring 2000 and have been there since. At New Hope, we got married, celebrated the birth of our son, Matthew, and dedicated him on Easter Sunday.

Occasionally on Sundays, Dan would share the day's Scripture reading with the children of the church and ask them to summarize the story. One morning, we read about how the disciples were terrified when Jesus came toward them, walking on water. In prompting the students to recount the story, he asked, "Why do you think the disciples were scared?"

"Bears!!!" Matthew immediately blurted out. At that, the adult sitting in front of our toddler son turned to him, smiled, and nodded in agreement; bears are indeed scary, and they would be even scarier walking on water.

We had just returned from Yosemite National Park, and Joan had been scrupulous about removing every conceivable object with a food-like scent from our vehicle, including fruity-smelling hair shampoo and mint toothpaste.[14] Joan's bear phobia was at such high alert that any slight rustle in the night had to come from a bear. Matthew picked up on Joan's paranoia, so he asked her point blank, in an utterly serious manner with wide eyes, "Mommy, are we going to be eaten by bears?" He evidently had no reason to believe his parents could protect him. This bear fear continued even when we returned to Oakland and were at church.

Sometimes our fears are rational, but other times they stem from anxieties and insecurities that arise deep within. Parenting raises those fears because we are thrust into the responsibility of protecting our children. Middle-class, helicopter parents—like Joan and I—hover over their sons and daughters who need SPF 500 sunscreen and cell phones with GPS to track them. We would wrap Matthew in Bubble Wrap if we could, but that's impractical. We like popping it too much.

The fears of helicopter parents for their children's safety are certainly legitimate. Furthermore, those living in low-income areas like we do face even scarier situations. Books about Tiger moms and Teddy Bear dads don't have anything to say about childrearing in this type of environment. Our community is certainly not conducive to a child's academic achievement, nor is it a protected place to explore his independence and autonomy.

One year, the *San Francisco Chronicle* newspaper covered Joan's work and life in East Oakland on its front page. The first lines read,

> In the past three years, two bullets shattered the front window, a teenager was shot just outside and the downstairs neighbor was mugged. Before that, a woman's lifeless body was unearthed from a trash bin less than a block away.
>
> But that part of East Oakland—where the neighborhoods of Fruitvale and San Antonio meet—is where Dr. Joan Jie-eun Jeung has chosen to live with her husband and their 6-year-old son.[15]

Since that time, similar events have occurred: a robber kicked down our front door to break in, and another time, a bullet knocked our dining room lampshade clear off. When the *Chronicle* readers learned about the location of our residential choice based on our faith and convictions, we were lambasted in the comments section. One person accused us of abusing our son by making him live in such unsafe circumstances. Another vilified us as those "crazy Korean Conservative Christian fanatics."

A normal response, if one had the financial resources to do so, would be to move to a safer neighborhood. But just as we hadn't moved out of Oak Park and instead stayed to organize and improve its conditions, we chose to remain in our community and keep the Murder Dubs as our home. Joan and I feel that our call is to make our neighborhood a place of shalom. We didn't want to secure just the health and well-being of our own nuclear family, but wanted to extend our notion of who our family includes. If our neighbors are part of our family, then we want our neighborhood to be better for them as well.

By developing family practices around community, we have tried to address Matthew's fear of bears and his parents' fear of crime and violence. While we aren't completely safe, we do find some protection, and we do have the opportunity to live out Scripture in some very concrete ways.

The first practice we employ as a family is simply to be part of a larger family, our church community. When Matthew was just eight years old, we were driving along I-880 in Oakland. We came through our neighborhood, the stretch between 16th Avenue and Fruitvale Avenue, which is considered the most graffitied area in California.[16] Ironically, Matthew remarked, "We live in the rich part of Oakland, don't we?"

He said so because of the wealth of friends and family nearby. At New Hope Covenant Church, a large percentage of its members live within two blocks of each of other and we interact daily. Matthew receives the blessings of this fellowship every day.

Since our church family are in such proximity to each other—we live in a condo above one church family and live next door to another—Matthew can call a friend to come upstairs and play anytime. At New Hope, whenever we need a minivan to borrow, extra ingredients for a community meal, or an adult to watch a kid for a while, church family are right beside us. We are on-call for anyone who needs an escort to their parked car at night or a pickup delivery from the taco stand a block away. On our church e-mail discussion group, not a week goes by without a request for something to be shared, such as a ride to the airport or a ¼-inch drill bit. One parent even asked if anyone had small farm animals available for her kid's birthday party. (I want to request to borrow a large bird of prey for my brother's surprise anniversary party, just to see how New Hopers respond.)

Our children have learned to be family to one another as well. When Kai, a new kindergartener at Think College Now (TCN) Elementary School, went out for his first recess, he ran out to find Sierra, a big fourth grader and the daughter of another New Hope family. The hamster-cheeked kid announced in his squeaky voice, "I'm ready to play now!" and Sierra promptly made sure he had little friends to play with.

"It was comforting that our community was looking after our son,"

Shauna, his mother, expressed. She continued to marvel at the support of the New Hope church family: "Whenever I couldn't pick up my kids, I'd text and I'd have five parents who would respond."

Similarly, when David, son of Carlos and Linda, transferred to Matthew's elementary school, Matthew did something he had never done before. He woke up early and urged me to hurry up to drive to school. "Why the rush?" I inquired.

"It's David's first day. I want to be there for him," Matthew replied.

That's the gift of our church family. Since we are so close in proximity, we can be there for one another.

The second practice of our family is to act as peacemakers in our community. Matthew and his friends are learning this lesson in concrete ways. Many kids in our neighborhood get bullied; in California, Asian American youth are the group most often racially harassed.[17] Consequently, Matthew's school regularly conducts anti-bullying campaigns. He's learned the three steps to stop bullying: (1) ignore the bully; (2) if bullying continues, ask the bully to stop; (3) if bullying still persists, tell an adult.

Unfortunately, standing up to a bully is difficult, especially because the victim is usually smaller and weaker than the bully. That's why we encourage Matthew to go one step further in stopping bullying. Not only should he ignore or protest when he is bullied, but he ought to intervene when he sees *someone else* being bullied. Just as we learn from our neighbors that "blessed are the poor," we have to trust that "blessed are the peacemakers, for they will be called children of God" (Matt. 5:9).

When his classmates are being mean or rough, Matthew has asked them to stop. Instead of minding his own business, he's making it his business to protect the welfare of others. Matthew is able to do so because while he's average-sized for his age, he has an unusually large, intimidating head. He's also verbal enough in English to negotiate interactions and order others around. When he's older and kids may get more physically violent, we probably will warn him to use judgment in such interventions. At this point, though, we want Matthew to be concerned for more than his personal boundaries; we want him to feel responsible for the safety of everyone in his surroundings.

The last family practice is to be caretakers of the community. God's shalom aims not only to reconcile individuals to himself and to each other, but to the entirety of creation. One Saturday morning, I told Matthew we were going out to clean the creek running down from the Oakland hills and through our neighborhood. He complained, "Why do we have to go clean it?!"

"To teach you to care about the environment," I responded with fatherly wisdom.

"But I already care about the environment!" he rejoined. "I don't have to go and clean it, too."

Just as you can't just preach peace but you have to make peace, you can't say you care about the environment and not do anything about it. When Oak Park Apartments was redesigned, the changes in tenant behavior, especially in how they took care of their surroundings, were stark. As they became more proud of their living conditions, the youth also felt better about themselves. We know that our environment shapes our lives; if we can transform our environment, we can also affect how our neighbors see themselves and their community.

Since living at Oak Park, Dan Schmitz has become the Johnny Appleseed of the neighborhood by planting numerous trees along surrounding blocks. Our backyard has a community garden where Mien grandmas provide us fresh produce—Southeast Asian vegetables such as mustard greens and *kabochas* (Thai pumpkins)—that are as locally grown as you can get. Along with our duplex co-owners, the Pascuals, we have installed solar panels on our roof. We also have gotten a plug-in hybrid Volt, so Joan and I can commute to work solely on renewable energy.

Along with these steps to steward our environment well, Matthew and I regularly go out into our neighborhood, rallying his church friends to come along, to sweep up litter, paint over graffiti, or join monthly peace walks. We don't make much of a noticeable dent in our community's appearance, but at least we're trying. After we paint over initials of graffiti artists, Matthew leaves a little paper note for them. He signed one letter: "Dear Mr. TS, Please stop painting graffiti in our neighborhood. From, the kids of Oakland." He says that vandalizing others' property is a sin, but that our love and painting over graffiti can cover up sin.[18] Since then, TS hasn't left his tag on our fences. Our hope is that as we beautify our environment, our neighbors will see their community, themselves, and others in ways that God designed.

When we're in Yosemite, we are aware of and respect bears. We thus take adequate precautions to stow our food so that once we do, we can enjoy the beauty of God. When we're in East Oakland, we do fear for our safety. We thus teach Matthew to rely on his community, work for peace in our community, and care for his community. Once he does, he can be called a child of God.

Critical Pedagogies: From Competition to Compassion

Besides fearing for Matthew's safety, Joan and I are obsessed about his education. Since we have strongly differing opinions about the role of education, we have ongoing debates over where he attends school. Joan is more of a Tiger mom, desiring Matthew to receive the best academic training possible. I am more of a lazy Teddy Bear dad and hope that Matthew doesn't get too much homework so that I don't have to supervise boring sessions of math drills. Instead, I'd rather have Matthew learn street skills that will enable him to mesh with a range of people. Schooling is not just about what you know, or even who you come to know; it's also about how you learn to deal with others.

This debate over our children's education also racks our New Hope church community. On one hand, adult children of immigrant parents highly value the academic opportunities afforded them. Their parents left everything, including their families in Asia, to come for their graduate studies in the United States. They sacrificed much so that their children could get the strongest education possible—admission into UC Berkeley, Stanford, Harvard. Joan reasons to me, "You and I went to the best public high schools in California. Who are we to deny the same opportunity to Matthew?" We may have chosen to live in East Oakland, she maintains, but we shouldn't sacrifice his future without his choice in the matter.

On the other hand, other parents take a missional approach to education. They feel that part of the calling toward social justice and equity must entail improving the state of public education, especially in poorly funded communities. The statistics are deplorable. If a child can't read by the third grade, the chances that he will be able to continue his learning drop dramatically; after third grade, students shift from learning to read to reading to learn. In Oakland, three in five students cannot read at grade level. At neighborhood schools in our zip code, the scores are even worse because we have more students learning English. If New Hope children attended the same school, perhaps the parents' concerted effort would not only help our own children's education, but that of the entire class as well.

After much hand wringing, New Hope families gave up trying to choose the same school for all our children. Some attended schools in the hills, where the families are wealthier and the test scores are higher, while others remained local in the flatlands, where we could walk our children to school.

Joan and I made a compromise when we chose school options for Matthew. For the school lottery, we listed only high-performing schools based on test scores.[19] However, our first choices were schools in the flatlands where the overwhelming majority of students were low income. I wanted Matthew to learn alongside a range of children who were both racially and economically diverse.

We also preferred for Matthew to be in schools with immigrant children. Children of Asian immigrant parents work hard because the students feel obligated to repay their debts to their parents. Matthew, in contrast, doesn't see Joan or me suffering much hardship on his behalf. Even though we try to look pained and long-suffering when we have to slice organic mangoes for him at breakfast, that sacrifice doesn't move him. Since we can't guilt him into working hard, we figured hanging around immigrant children might give him peer motivation.

New Hope parents Albert and Shauna have the same ideas in sending their children to our local public school. Just as Albert's parents gifted him with a strong educational background, Albert wants to be a gift to our neighborhood and invest in Think College Now (TCN) Elementary School, where his children attend. Since the school had lost major funding, Albert took the initiative to share about this school's achievements, especially in educating low-income Latino children, to his parents and the broader Taiwanese community. Understanding the value of investing in the community as well as in their "own" children, Albert's network raised tens of thousands of dollars for TCN. New Hope also donated thousands, even though most of our members do not have children at the school.

Alejandro, another New Hope member, also sends his children to TCN and shared how his son, Mario, who is Matthew's age, has been affected by his classmates. At one open house, Mario noticed that his friend in his work group looked disconsolate. After inquiring, he learned that this friend's father had been just recently deported, which upset him because his dad could not attend the school event.

What was worse was that his friend's mother was pregnant. Without their father, the family worried about simply finding transport to the hospital, let alone paying for rent and groceries.

Troubled, Mario asked his dad why his friend's father was deported. Alejandro explained that some adults do not have the proper documents to stay in the United States, so authorities arrest some of them and split apart families.

Then Alejandro explained that Mario's own mother didn't have legal authorization to stay in the United States, either. With the chilling fear that he could be separated from his own parent at any time,

Mario felt even more connected to his friend and paid special attention to him.

In our community, Mario receives firsthand education about how to care for the alien. Similarly, Matthew learns about how to look after the orphan, because he meets these individuals on a regular basis.

Joan and I became trained as foster parents, so occasionally the Catholic Charities agency would ask us to act as respite parents. When the regular foster parents of a young person needed a break, we were certified to host their children for a weekend. Through this program, we got to meet some amazing young people, ranging from youth who escaped North Korea to individuals trafficked across borders. One such youth was Thanh.

At the age of twelve, Thanh had to leave his parents' hometown in Vietnam to search for work to support his family. He first found a job on a coffee plantation in the south, and later found his way up north to Hanoi, the capital. Paying $300 of his own up front, he was able to sign a labor contract with a Chinese fishing vessel. At the end of three years, he was to be paid $900—quite a sum for a boy age sixteen.

The work on the ship was grueling, since they had to catch and unload fish for eighteen hours a day. Thanh complained of working— waist-deep—in squid that he had to shovel into crates. The labor was also dangerous. Thanh revealed to us a six-inch scar on his calf where an eight-foot-long shark bit him after it had landed on the ship's deck. A fellow crew member drowned when he fell into the fishing nets and couldn't disentangle himself.

When his ship was fishing in Alaskan waters, it was stopped by the U.S. Coast Guard. The Coast Guard returned the fishermen to their native countries, but they detained Thanh. Since he was still a minor, he was considered a victim of human trafficking. When his parents were informed that he could remain in the U.S. and even get a visa for his sister, they asked him to stay even though he wanted to return home.

At the age of seventeen, Thanh came to stay at our home for a few days. That weekend, we took him to our cousin's anniversary celebration, a luau. Noting the casual atmosphere, Thanh relaxed a bit and acted more like himself. He lit a cigarette, popped open a beer, and enjoyed the hula performance after a trip to the buffet line.

My aunts and uncles began to murmur, "Who's the kid smoking with Matthew?" So I had to inform Thanh, "Hey, in America, kids aren't supposed to smoke and drink yet." Thanh was surprised. He explained, "On the ship, we always ate this kind of fish with beer."

Once Thanh stubbed out his cigarette, Matthew and I realized that this kid was a salty old sea dog who had already experienced much more of life than the normal American teenager. In fact, he had seen a lot more than I had in my fifty years. Thanh's resilience amazes us to this day, and we've learned grit from other foster kids as they've also shared their own harrowing stories.

This type of education that Matthew is receiving—relating to others humbly and developing an empathy for others' struggles—isn't what I was taught at Stanford University. When I wondered what I would do with my degree, my advisor told me, "It doesn't matter what you study. Just be the best and you'll get a job." We were expected to be the best, to do better than others, and everything would follow.[20]

I learned to compete at Stanford, but I didn't learn to be compassionate. In fact, I rue that one of my major lessons from that school was how to be entitled. Alexia Salvatierra, a community organizer who worked in Oakland, explained that Jesus often healed lepers who had lost feeling for parts of their bodies. She said that Jesus still needs to heal lepers today, because the church has lost feeling for parts of its body—those who are poor, those who are marginalized.[21] This type of leprosy of non-compassion is contagious, especially at places like Stanford University.

That's why Joan and I raise Matthew in East Oakland, to inoculate him from the leprosy of indifference. As he learns to relate to others without his privilege and as he lives among those without his power, Matthew receives lessons that you can't receive at world-class universities.

I have delighted in Matthew so much—perhaps in the way my great-grandfather, Jeung Quong Chong loved kids—that I wanted an even larger family.

Fostering a Spirit of Openness

After having Matthew, Joan and I tried for five years to have another child, but with no success. Since I was so enthusiastic and insistent about the idea of foster parenting, Joan agreed to explore the possibility and even went through the foster parent training process. Yet after learning of the difficult experiences of other foster parents and reading about the attachment issues of foster children, she balked.

Then, seemingly out of the blue but clearly in some providential plan, Catholic Charities staff called us and asked if we would take in two sisters from Burma. The girls had already been in the United States for a year, and the staff felt that they could really flourish in our care. Most important, the social workers had met with them regularly and could assure us that they weren't axe murderers. Wouldn't we like to change a life and foster a refugee child? Or two?

At this point, foster parenting wasn't just an abstract possibility; it became a concrete opportunity. The stories of the two girls, who were orphaned in Burma and then had to flee its oppressive conditions, weren't presented just as compelling stories, but as the lived experiences of individuals who could become our daughters. We had only two weeks to decide whether or not we wanted to become a family.

We quickly assembled our New Hope church family members to pray for us. Since we lived so closely and intimately together, these people would automatically become foster aunts and uncles if the girls were to join us. This decision wasn't just a Jeung family matter, but a church matter about how we would love and serve one another.

The Sunday before we had to make our decision, Joan had a vision during Communion. God spoke to her: "I've invited these girls to my banquet table. Is there room for them at yours?" Tearfully, she had to run to the bathroom just to get some privacy and compose herself. I never get these strong, heartfelt calls from above to wrestle with my convictions. I just get tantalized by visions of fun-filled adventures, such as taking kids on family vacations to Disneyland. As long as the kids in question aren't axe murderers, I allow myself to pursue these escapades, such as moving into Oak Park or becoming a foster parent.

Responding to a message from God, Joan added two more to our family. Bethsy and Bonny, ages seventeen and fifteen, came to join our family just three weeks after we first heard of them; that's a pretty short pregnancy.

Welcome to America: Another Type of Education

When they first arrived in the United States, the two girls walked off the airplane with one suitcase each and no money. As young girls, they had left Burma with their older sister and fled to Malaysia, where they would gain refugee status. Even though they had to drop out of school and began working in a Japanese restaurant, they marveled at their new life in that country. Bonny, the younger sister, recalled taking hot showers for hours because of its novelty. Bethsy reported that they would eat only ice cream for meals, because they had never had it in Burma. After living in some harrowing conditions on their own for two years, they received a notice from the United Nations refugee agency that they were to come in for blood tests. Bethsy said they didn't know at the time, but they were being immediately resettled as unaccompanied minors somewhere in California. Their older sister, who did not have the capacity to care for them, moved to the state of Georgia.

Bethsy and Bonny first lived for a year in Hercules, a Bay Area suburb, but then their social workers reassigned them to live with us. Coming to our home didn't seem to be that difficult a transition for them. They quickly set up their own rooms, learned their way around Oakland by bus, and got settled into their new school. Like other

American teens, they texted their friends, updated their Facebook and Instagram accounts, and watched Netflix late into the night.

The speed of their acculturation was amazing. On our first drive through San Francisco, Bonny looked around at the city skyline and asked me tons of questions with the curiosity of an anthropology graduate student, "How much do cars cost? . . . How do they afford to build such big buildings? . . ." I went on and on explaining American economics and sociology as clearly as possible. Some things about America, though, just aren't that easy to grasp and assimilate . . . or even to explain. Bonny wondered, "Why is Paris Hilton so famous?" That question, for example, had me stumped.

While Bonny was enamored by American pop culture, Bethsy was amazed by the political freedom in the United States. We marched in one of the first Occupy protests in 2011, and she commented, "You couldn't do this in Burma." When she was twelve years old, Bethsy and her friends organized their classmates to clean the town's only park. That evening, she was called in by public security officials because their community service constituted an act of "unlawful assembly." Fortunately, their church pastor intervened on behalf of the youth, and she did not get into further trouble.

Despite the girls' eagerness to adopt American ways, integrating into American life and, especially, into our family, had its bumps. Again, education became the major concern of our parenting.

Bethsy entered her American high school at the age of sixteen after having her schooling interrupted for three years. Even though she was very studious, acquiring English skills to pass the California High School Exit Exam (CAHSEE) proved almost impossible in such a short time. She realized that she could not learn English quickly enough in order to graduate, so she made the rational decision to drop out, like many other immigrant English learners. These high stakes tests actually discourage many students from learning, albeit unintentionally.

When Bethsy came to us, we encouraged her to reenter school to obtain her high school diploma. Oakland has an International High

School designed for students just like her, those who had arrived in the United States recently and would be likely to drop out if they didn't have a rigorous English curriculum.

A question from Bethsy's English essay exit exam demonstrates how this test may be unfair to certain populations. The essay question asked, "What would you do with a million dollars?" For middle-class students who have money and experience spending it, answering this question is easy. They might travel; they might purchase cars; or they might buy homes. Bethsy, however, had difficulty thinking of what to buy and could not begin to imagine having this amount of money. Having just arrived from Malaysia where she had been living with eight people in a small apartment without a kitchen, she didn't spend her time dreaming about spending millions. She focused on surviving day to day. Although Bethsy might be able to compose a coherent essay, she didn't have the cultural or socioeconomic background to pass such a test.

Our bumbling parenting didn't help the girls with their educational issues, either. After a few months of living with us, I noticed that Bethsy wasn't wearing her glasses. When I asked her about them, she said she had lost them a month prior.

For weeks, Bethsy was nearly blind, couldn't see her classroom whiteboard well (she proactively sat in the front row), and must have lived in a fuzzy haze. I felt horrible about being blind myself to Bethsy's nearsightedness. She hadn't felt comfortable telling us her needs, so we weren't even aware of them.

Too often, we in the United States are blind to the newcomers around us and to their struggles to adapt. With the allure of its economic status, pop culture, and political freedom, the United States draws those seeking better opportunities. Bethsy's example, though, illustrates how difficult it is for newcomers to integrate fully into the United States. Fortunately, she persevered and finally passed the CAHSEE after her eighth attempt. Her immigrant classmates who don't pass, in contrast, will probably be relegated low-paying, service-sector jobs or unemployment.

Matthew, on the other hand, quickly learned how to be open to others when Bethsy and Bonny moved in. At dinner one night, he said that he would never get married because he wanted to live with us. Joan replied that if he did not get a wife, he would not be able to have children and have his own family.

"That's okay," he responded. "I can just get foster people."

As a child, Matthew has learned to easily welcome and embrace the aliens and strangers in our midst. Joan and I still needed some lessons.

Moving Boundaries: From Independence to Interdependence

Welcoming Bethsy and Bonny into our home as our guests seemed easy in comparison to becoming a family where we are their parents and they are our daughters. Joining a family with set routines—such as family meals at breakfast and dinner, Saturday movie nights, and church meetings on Friday evenings and Sunday mornings—they found their places at the table quite comfortably. Making enough waffles for everyone at breakfast took a bigger toaster and a little more time, but we all adjusted. Eating at home even became a fine dining experience. Bethsy and Bonny were so quick to take our dishes at the end of the meal and wash them that I felt as if we lived on a cruise ship with multiple servers waiting on us. Just when we got our family routines down, however, my Panda vision for our little family got rocked by a new challenge. Making our household a "home" to Bethsy and Bonny proved quite difficult after all.

Bonny's English improved so much by the end of her sophomore year that her teachers felt she would be better challenged at a small high school in our neighborhood. She entered Life Academy, a high school that focused on health and science and had the highest UC and California State University acceptance rate of any Oakland high school. Since it had only about seventy students per grade, Bonny received close, personal attention. She thrived academically and obtained a prized internship at a nearby hospital. Though she was able to succeed in her own school work, tragedy struck her classmates.

In November of her junior year, Life Academy students were informed that a recent graduate of the school had been shot to death outside a friend's house. The next month, the five-year-old brother of a Life Academy student was killed in a drive-by shooting while at a taco stand with his family. Even as Bonny and our family participated in a fast for a season of peace, the violence that shook the school continued.

In June, just before school got out for the summer, Bonny's classmate was gunned down while standing outside a grocery store. His seat was right behind hers in math class, and she remembers how they would joke around during group work. This student leader, who wanted to become a probation officer, had been a model of how the school helped turn students around. Appallingly, he was the sixth student of Life Academy to be killed during its seven years of existence.

Bonny, like her classmates, was traumatized to have to attend two funerals in one school year. Warned not to wear certain gang colors during the memorial service, she and her classmates walked arm-in-arm down the streets of Oakland toward a wake when they should have been jogging in P.E. class. Her country of birth, Burma, has seen the longest-running civil war of over sixty years, yet she was not prepared for the wanton violence of Oakland. She recalled how sad her classmates were. Then she discussed how she felt going to school: "I didn't feel really safe, especially when I took the bus. There were a lot of drunk people who asked me for money. And one old lady on the corner would always shout at people."

Even I, who had lived in East Oakland for twenty years, began to feel unsafe on the streets for the first time. When I attended Bonny's end-of-the-year school performance, I thought about the danger presented by simply standing beside a young man in Oakland. One might be the mistaken target of a gang, and anyone around him could be accidently shot in a drive-by. That year, Oakland had averaged five to six persons shot daily.[22] Like Jeremiah, we mourned that because of Oakland's gun violence, "Death has climbed in through our windows and has entered our fortresses; it has removed the children from the streets and the young men from the public squares" (Jer. 9:21).

Bonny shared her fears with her caseworker, who quite understandably had her client's safety as her top priority. Bonny said she wanted to move out of Oakland. When the worker asked her about leaving us and Bethsy, Bonny remained adamant about getting out of Oakland even if she had to be on her own. The caseworker proceeded to locate another family for Bonny.

When the caseworker finally told us about this situation in early August, Joan and I were shocked, then angered. As Bonny's parents, we felt we should have been consulted before a move was to be made. Had we known about her concerns, we would have sought more counseling, considered transferring schools, or even had gotten her self-defense classes. Now she was being separated from our family by the foster care system.

"The worst day in my life was the day the social worker came," my uncle lamented when he had to leave his sisters and move to a group home. As I recalled my mother's and uncle's traumatizing experience, I became even more infuriated at how the system can tear apart families.

Part of the problem is that this foster care system is based on a Eurocentric family model that prioritizes the child's independence and autonomy over all else. The white caseworker believed that Bonny needed to learn to make her own decisions regarding her own safety and future.

Bethsy and Bonny, however, had spent most of their lives on their own already. They didn't necessarily need the freedom of independence. I felt that they needed the security of interdependence. Joan and I wanted them to become attached to us and others, to become open to help and support, and to learn to make decisions as a family. Although self-sufficiency is critical to learn, so is attachment to others.

The girls had enough experience of being on their own. They were orphaned as young children and had to survive as exploited child laborers. We wanted them to have a different experience, that of being loved and supported by a family.

After much prayer and discussion, Joan and I offered Bonny another option besides staying in Oakland or leaving for another foster home. Instead of Bonny moving out, we would all move with her. We decided to leave East Oakland, my cherished community where I had made my home for decades, so that our new family could remain intact.

So much for our call to our neighborhood, our intentional practices of community and compassion, our solidarity with the poor. All that I preached and hoped to practice was pushed to the side as we prioritized our daughter in this family crisis.

With only a month before the start of the school semester, we scrambled to find a home in Alameda, a suburb adjacent to Oakland. Fortunately, we found a house that we could afford with the financial support of my sister and mother. Within a matter of weeks, we packed up all our belongings and relocated. I was truly Hakka and a guest person after all.

Epilogue: Chinese Love Languages

We spent a year in Alameda so that Bonny could attend high school there. At the same time, Bethsy and Matthew continued going to school in Oakland, so we spent a lot of time chauffeuring our kids. Living in the suburbs was a drastic change; we never got to know any of our neighbors, but I did spend a lot of time gawking at their garages. Unlike Oaklanders, Alamedans felt safe enough to leave their garage doors open. Their two-car garages were so chock-full of stuff that they couldn't fit their cars inside them. In contrast, we didn't have enough furniture to fill our new home.

As parents, Joan and I feel obligated to provide our children with a sense of safety, a strong education, and most importantly, a reverence for God.[23] Raising families in Oakland certainly has its challenges, especially given the violence and the poor quality of public schools in our neighborhood. Yet it also provides great opportunities for us to teach our family about Chinese Panda love.

Western conceptions of love seem individualistic to me. Christian therapists recommend that married couples must love as a self-conscious choice and need to express that love in the specific ways their partner understands. Panda love from China, though, assumes the primacy of others and the group is foremost. Marriage isn't based on meeting individual needs, but on a steadfast loyalty and faithfulness to the relationship. It's reflective of God's *hesed*, his loving-kindness that is new every morning, to us.

Likewise, Western parenting focuses on socializing a child as an individual, with values for autonomy, independence, and freedom. Parental love, then, is expressed as nurture of a child's self-esteem and encouragement of the child's personal responsibility. These are important traits, but Panda love inculcates other values and expresses itself in different ways. The languages of Chinese Panda love are food and sacrifice.

The Chinese word for filial piety—that is, respect for one's parents, elders, and ancestors—is *xiao*. In this character, a component signifying the elder is placed above a component for a child. The child therefore supports the elder while the elder takes responsibility for the child. It represents the mutual interdependence prized in Asian families.

Chinese parental love, then, takes the form of sacrificial provision for the children's physical well-being and for their future. For example, I love cooking for the family, eating breakfast and dinner together daily, and purchasing special snacks for each of our kids. I get a huge kick out of being responsible for their material needs. Surprisingly, food isn't identified as one of the primary love languages, yet that's probably how 1.7 billion Chinese show their love. Even God uses food as a love language; he invites us to his banqueting table and offers Jesus as our daily rice.

Just as food is one love language of Asians, sacrifice is another. Asian immigrant parents willingly and often unthinkingly make huge sacrifices for their children. They often leave their homelands, become mute and deaf in a new society, experience downward mobility and lowered status, and work long, wearying hours so their children can have opportunities in the United States. Seeing their parents' struggles, Asian American children tend to feel very obligated and motivated to live up to their parents' expectations. I think that's also why Asian American second-generation Christians can be so fervent in their faith. They understand God's sacrifice in deep, personal ways because they have family models of this self-giving.

As children are surrounded by this type of love, they learn to rely on the support of their family to always be there. They also find great meaning in giving back to their family, even more than any personal fulfillment.

Feeling safer in Alameda, Bonny graduated and was able to get accepted to UC Santa Cruz. This achievement is pretty remarkable, considering she only got a fourth-grade education in Burma, had to learn English, and received just four years of American secondary schooling. Beyond getting a start on her education and career during that time, Bonny also learned a lesson about interdependence.

She explains, "It's good I didn't have to move in with another family to start all over again. I felt really supported—I think Joan and Russell would do anything for me."

Bethsy eventually moved out of state for work and to spend time with other family members. On a recent Father's Day, though, she surprised me by coming back and moving home. In a card she wrote, "I'm so thankful for helping me when I needed help, [which was] all the time! Thank you for letting me be a part of your life." We started as hosts and guests in the same house. Over time, God made us a family as we became interdependent, integral parts of each other's lives.

In China, orphaned pandas are cared for by animal scientists who become panda foster parents. The scientists don furry panda outfits to feed the animals. The hope is that the baby pandas will attach to them as pandas and won't get accustomed to being with humans. Mind you, these scientists walk around in these suffocating suits in Sichuan province, known as one of the furnaces of China for its sweltering summer heat.

This nourishing, sacrificial, and loyal Panda love is how God loves us. He came in human form, walked among us, and suffered for our sake so that we can be reconciled as a new people. Even when we may reject this love, he continues to provide, care, and give. Ultimately, his sacrifice teaches us how we, adopted into his family, are to live similarly. May we foster the same type of self-emptying and long-devoted hearts for each other, as we are members of God's larger family.

CHAPTER 6

The Call as the Church in Exile

When we moved back from Alameda to Oakland in 2012, we were excited to return full swing into things. Matthew once again had playdates with kids from around the block. Bethsy had moved out on her own in Oakland while Bonny commenced her studies at college. Joan and others started a neighborhood tutoring program, where we used five rooms in our house to seat all the students and tutors. I became council chair of New Hope Covenant Church, and we wanted to launch new discipleship ministries to develop local leaders.

Once our church year began, though, a crisis bowled us over. For the first time in its ten-year history, our church preschool had enrolled enough students to break even. But then a personnel incident occurred where we had to act swiftly for the sake of the students. We struggled to replace a popular staff member and to assure the parents of their children's welfare.

In the middle of dealing with this emergency, the church council received news that threatened the life of the congregation. Some long-time members expressed grave dissatisfaction regarding the abilities of church leadership. A few councilmembers were deeply wounded by the tone of dissension and others felt personally betrayed. Some of us expressed feeling ripped apart on the inside, as if we were children torn between divorcing parents. The wounds of the conflict were so raw that some people couldn't bear to be in the same room as others.

We had built our church on the hope of reconciliation—to be redeemed to God and to be in close community with one another. Many of us sacrificed prime adult years to reach out to the community, disciple young persons, and establish the communal practices that shaped our church. I did not care much about my own career ambitions, but instead had always tried to focus on what will last eternally, especially God's people, the church. Now, our congregation seemed to be imploding over petty issues of personality and of strategy. The conflict often woke me up in the middle of the night. When I could not return to sleep, I prayed over my anger about others' complaints and gossiping. I also needed to repent of my own complaints and gossip.

To help reestablish unity, the church council planned a leaders' appreciation night for the entire church. We rented the neighborhood's fanciest meeting place and arranged a reception that featured our best homemade desserts. As we expressed gratitude for the gifting and service of each leader, Matthew and other children honored them with leis.

Thirty minutes into the program, a church member came running in from outside yelling, "Jose's been hit by a car!" Jose, our church youth director, had been helping to push a stalled truck to the curb when another pickup truck slammed into him. He lay crumpled as Joan cradled him in her arms until the ambulance arrived. The children were quickly ushered into another space, and the church body began praying earnestly for his life.

That night, however, Jose passed away. My worst fear about living in Oakland, what we parents dread the most, had been realized. One of our own, innocent family members had been killed by violence on our streets. The driver who hit Jose was high on crystal meth and alcohol. As I had to phone other church leaders with the news, my heart was wrenched again and again.

Acting as a Good Samaritan, Jose was helping a stranded traveler on the roadside. He was just about to complete a three-month challenge in which he would serve anyone who needed assistance before himself. Bonny and the New Hope teenagers to whom he ministered will always miss his infectious joy and corny riddles.

The following week, Bethsy was mugged outside her apartment. When she initially resisted, the mugger hit her with a gun. Instead of complying, she got angry and fought back even more. The guy repeatedly butted her to get at her purse, but finally he ran away. Bethsy was left bruised with a slight concussion. Tired of constantly having to watch her surroundings in Oakland, she moved out of state soon thereafter to join other family members.

Like many at New Hope, I was devastated. We had lost so many to the streets of Oakland and had little to show for our efforts. Our beloved community was being ripped apart from the inside and out. My family had been broken up, and my soul was beaten down. I had felt called here, but to what and for what?

Vocational Calling: Reaching Your Potential and Letting Your Voice Speak?

God's calling can be understood in two ways. His calling is a summons from a high authority, which we are ordered to follow. This summons involves an important task, such as delivering a royal message, and we receive the power of that authority to complete it. God's calling is also an invitation from a gracious host. God invites us to his banqueting table, where we are requested to join with him and others to share and celebrate our close relationship. When we think of our work or occupation, we tend to think of the first sense of calling, that of being destined for important tasks.

One year after graduating with a master's degree from Stanford University, I found myself working a temp job at a roller skate factory in

San Francisco's Bayview district. I stood all day, filing invoices. It took only one hour of mind-numbing repetition to make me question, "What on earth am I going to do with my life?" Even though I was fortunate to have a job in which I could "skate by," I saw myself as one of the Hebrew slaves in Egypt, toiling to make bricks from a few straws.

The idea that God had called me to something special and important tantalized me, especially when compared to being a dull cog in a factory making boots with wheels. As the youngest child from Hakka peasantry and raised by ghettoized parents, I was well-versed in my family's pursuit of something more. And as someone who grew up watching Broadway musicals and Super Bowl champions, the dream that I could play an important and significant role for God enthralled me. It enticed me, but it also haunted me; when I compared myself to my classmates from Lowell High and Stanford University and their early achievements, I felt burdened by my seemingly unreached potential. If only I could discern my calling, then perhaps I could fulfill my destiny.

In search of this calling, I read books such as *What Color Is Your Parachute?* and found that my parachute was orange, which I didn't think really matched my bronze skin tone.[1] Other Christian books on vocation and calling were not much more helpful. They each suggested that I should find the job suited to my unique passions and gifts. That just irked me, because I remained in the roller skate industry, and it wasn't remotely close to the field of my career dreams.

In his book entitled *Courage and Calling: Embracing Your God-Given Potential*, seminary president Gordon Smith claims that each of us has a *unique* calling from God to follow. In fact, he asserts that God has gifted each of us with the potential to serve, and nothing is more important than being courageous in pursuing what God has asked us to do.[2] Another author suggests that not only does each of us have God-given potential, but we also should express who we are through our work. According to Palmer Parker, a Quaker educator on spirituality and social change, we need to listen to the inner voices of what we value the most and what we want to be about. Our life's work should then express these ultimate hopes and critical ideals.[3]

Even those who emphasize God's plan for a new kingdom—instead of focusing on individual desires—write that we need to maximize our personal talents and strengths. Amy Sherman, *Christianity Today* Book of the Year award winner in the category of Christian Living, writes that the righteous are those who steward their job positions and use their expertise for the disadvantaged. At the same time, she also aims to help readers find their vocational sweet spot, "the place where our gifts and passions intersect with God's priorities and the world's needs."[4]

Without intending to, these books inflated my grandiose desire to become the protagonist of my own action hero movie. God has a great plan to save the world, and I play a special role in that story! All I had to do was figure out my potential and passions in order to discern what job God had for me. Then I just needed the courage to pursue it.

I wanted to pattern myself after Moses, Esther, or Daniel—leaders who made a difference for their oppressed people. When I was at Stanford, I vividly remember a talk about Moses given by a former gymnast on the U.S. Olympics team. He shared that, like Stanford students, Moses had received the best education possible, and that was while he was being raised in the pharaoh's court. In an apparent waste of his training, he had to spend forty years as a shepherd before he led the Israelites out of Egypt. However, the point of the talk was that we, like Moses, need to learn humility by spending time in the wilderness. This lesson about our character was relevant, yet the talk also had an implicit assumption. Once we learned to be humble servant leaders, we Stanford students had the potential to be—and were expected to become—great leaders like Moses.

Persons of great education and power have the opportunity to discern their vocational calling and to pursue careers of their own choosing. I have this privilege and continue to wrestle with discerning God's call on my life. I dream with Joan about going on exciting mission trips where lives are transformed. I plan with Dan Schmitz and others in my neighborhood to build community institutions that revitalize the city. I long to be needed and useful to a racial movement through which real, lasting change is made.

After all my years in Oakland, these dreams remain. What has changed, though, is my sense of my own, individual role.

I do not believe God has gifted me with the potential for a special job or task uniquely meant for me, especially in regard to the work that I do. How can I make such presumptions when, throughout history, the overwhelming majority of people toiled in the fields? For the millions who have worked as slaves in past times, and for the millions who are modern-day slaves, can we argue that their work is part of God's plan, or that their potential was simply not embraced by them?

My great-grandmother, Hall Gock Tie, certainly didn't have many choices for work as a young Chinese migrant girl in Point Alones, California. As an undocumented worker, Hop Shue, my grandfather, probably did not find his life expressed fully in his job as a fish peddler. The courage to find one's "vocational sweet spot" hardly applies to the day-laborers at Oak Park or the girls trafficked on the streets down the block from my home. They need courage simply to find work.

So, rather than looking to highly educated, white authors for career counseling, I began looking to those around me—people of color and the disadvantaged—to see how God led them in their work. I needed alternative role models of those who pursued their calling, and I found one right in my own home.

Vocational Calling: Lessons from Feminists of Color

My mother, Bernice Jeung, offered me another understanding about work. Perhaps it is not as self-fulfilling, expressive, or world changing, but her attitude toward vocation is still as noble a perspective as that of the just-cited European American writers. Mom labored for forty-five years as an X-ray technician. As a woman of color in the 1940s, she initially couldn't find a job in her profession. Fortunately, she eventually was hired by one of the first female radiologists in San Francisco, who understood the workplace challenges faced by women and gave her a chance.

Standing on her feet all day, Mom told people to hold their breath and not to move until the X-ray was complete. (Ironically, whenever we photographed her, she couldn't take her own advice and she'd flinch. Shots of Mom are often blurred and we have hundreds of photos of her with her eyes shut.) For decades, she repeated the same words and went through the same motions. She wasn't paid much, and ten years of her salary went to pay for my four-year, private university tuition.

When I asked about her work, she nonchalantly replied that she did what she always had to do. Growing up during the Depression, she worked as a teenager picking strawberries to help her family pay the bills. She assumed full responsibility for her three younger siblings when her mother was hospitalized. Just months after she was married, she was saddled with having to take care of her husband's younger siblings when her father-in-law passed away suddenly. She then had her own children and took in her mother, who was recovering from a heart attack. For almost all of her life, my mother worked in order to take care of her family. That was the noble, selfless meaning found in her vocation.

In her retirement, my mother still volunteers her time for others when she's not playing mah-jong. She files for a homeless clinic and plays games with the elderly at a nearby senior residential facility. Some of the elderly whom she helps are twenty years younger than she! We joke that she needs to be careful when she leaves, because the caretakers might mistake her for a dementia patient trying to escape. She says she gives back so much because she received much from others, such as the Methodist church ladies who drove her siblings to visit her and my grandmother in the hospital.

My mother's Chinese work ethic finds its source in Confucian philosophies about human plasticity and relational ethics. Confucius believed that through self-cultivation, one can mold one's character because it is plastic and malleable. Virtue does not come from one's natural ability or innate capacity, but from one's single-minded effort and disciplined practice. This self-cultivation through hard work translates into other areas of one's life as well. Chinese who toil diligently—many are incorrigibly lazy, of course—do so because they believe they can garner results even when faced with bad luck, handicaps, or hardships. Confucian ethics also center on loyalty and reciprocity to the group. One's efforts are for the collective good of the whole, including that of future generations. Work is therefore not an expression of an individual's own passions and values, but of one's persistent dedication to loving one's family and community.

In addition, my mom's work ethic stems from her childhood poverty. Without any financial resources or land, she had only her human capital—that is, her own efforts and skills—to rely on. She therefore worked hard, like many other Chinese women.

This Chinese understanding of work—to work hard and to work for others—may better match biblical perspectives about one's labor than the books I read on vocational calling. If one reviews the proverbial "wife of noble character" in light of her work and not her marital status, one can identify what makes her noble. Her nobility stems from her diligence and self-sacrificial efforts.

Proverbs 31 discusses the conscientious attitude with which the person of "noble character" works. Like my mother, this worker toils diligently, with "eager hands." Whatever her work, she does so to the best of her ability.

The passage then examines for whom this person works. The noble worker toils first to provide for her family and others in her household (v. 15).[5] Secondly, she labors so that she can share resources with those who cannot help themselves: "She opens her arms to the poor and extends her hands to the needy" (v. 20). Likewise, the New Testament reminds us that we are to earn money so that we can support those in need (Eph. 4:28). Generosity and taking responsibility for others are the concerns of her work.

Finally, we read of the fruits of this woman's labor. Her work for others clothes her "with strength and dignity" in that she does not have to worry about the future (Prov. 31:25). The noble worker receives honor from children, praise from her spouse, and respect from the broader community as she works to give. Her nobility rests in how she relates to others, not in the work itself.

Tragically, work in and of itself has become alienating for most people. It may be sheer drudgery, as it was for me at the roller skate factory, or worse yet, it may be forced labor, as it is for millions who are trafficked. Unfortunately, this alienation from our own work seems to be the consequence of humanity's brokenness. Labor exploitation of workers and discrimination in the workplace, which my grandparents and parents faced, demonstrate this brokenness as well. In contrast, God created us in his image and aimed for our work to be creative and good, just as his work in creation was deemed very good.[6] His intention is also to make our work enjoyable and for our own self-sufficiency.[7]

One way that God redeems us from our alienation from our work is by imputing it—whatever the task is—with eternal significance. St. Paul exhorts slaves to hold to this belief: "Whatever you do, work at it with all our heart, as working for the Lord, not for human masters, since you know that you will receive an inheritance from the Lord as a reward" (Col. 3:23–24). Unlike me, God favors filing invoices at a roller skate factory as much as he honors the work of Daniel and Esther in the royal courts. Amazingly, he sanctifies labor that is despised by the world—even the back-breaking toil of Hakka in the fields—and considers it a rich offering that can bring pleasure to the Creator of the Universe.

If we are freed from the burden of finding the specific vocation to express and fulfill ourselves, then the process of discerning one's work and career becomes much less anxiety-ridden and self-absorbed. When we see how God intends work to be creative rather than alienating, then we can imagine labor that works toward the support and liberation of others.

Choosing to Become Men
and Women for Others

It took me nine years to complete a doctorate at UC Berkeley because I worked part-time, but mostly because I preferred to spend time hanging out with Oak Park folks. I also had fits and starts in my own interest in my research, which interrogated the symbolic boundaries and narrative discourses of religiously inspired organic intellectuals. The academic jargon of my own writing boggled even me, so the dissertation took a while.

Eventually, I found a way to finish my doctoral dissertation, and I tested the job market to see if God might call me elsewhere. We had just settled the Oak Park lawsuit, and it seemed that I was free to begin a new chapter in my life. Now serious in our relationship, Joan said she was willing to follow me wherever I chose to go. That gift certainly opened up possibilities.

One university in Colorado offered me an attractive, secure tenure-track position with research funding. If my calling was to pursue theoretical interests in a highly academic setting, that would have been the place to be. A Christian college in Pennsylvania recruited me as a sociologist to train its students in social justice and urban ministries. If I wanted to express my life in fighting for the marginalized, there I could have taken leadership within the evangelical world. Each job offer would have utilized my training and passions, and each had its own attractive trajectory.

You would think that some of the biggest decisions of my life—what to do and where to go for my career—would have been nerve-wracking, especially after I was presented with two great options. But in fact, the decisions were relatively easy for me to make. I turned down both options without any regret.

My third alternative was better: I chose to be with the people I loved.

My relationships at Oak Park, my church at New Hope, my ties to the youth of the Murder Dubs, and my family in the Bay Area were far more important to me than anything a job could offer. I am not suggesting that one's individual vocation is not important or that one's career should not be taken seriously. I am only saying that love for others is a strong reason to do anything and provides a helpful guide in decision-making. Obviously, with this love comes costs and hardships, but we are commanded to love first and foremost.

After deciding to stay in East Oakland with Joan and New Hope, I obtained a job at a community college an hour away. Later, I got a position at San Francisco State University where I am blessed to integrate my love for teaching and research with my concerns for low-income communities of color. To conduct needs assessments, my students and I organize events such as reunions for laid-off garment factory workers and health fairs for marginalized newcomers from Bhutan, Burma, and Mongolia. We even hosted a luau and boat dance for immigrant English-learners. As we drew these groups together, we gathered critical data about their needs and issues so that community groups can better advocate for them.

Of course, I appreciate that my work as a professor involves being a party host. That fits uniquely well with my personality and interests. Perhaps more significant, though, is that my job enables me to maintain my relationships and become responsible and generous, the hallmarks of the proverbial noble wife and the virtuous Confucian individual.

With our incomes, Joan and I can take care of our family and welcome in others. Our work also gives us the opportunities to be generous with our resources and time at New Hope and the Murder Dubs. Early on, Joan and I had a conviction that beyond our tithes, we ought to give away at least the same amount that we spend on our own enjoyment, such as vacations and eating out. Most years, we have given away as much as we have paid on our home mortgage. In living simply so that we can be hospitable and charitable, we have been able to help establish our New Hope preschool, finance a neighbor's purchase of their own first home, support missionaries inside and outside of the U.S., and assist young men out of debt and into financial freedom.

My college roommates recently had a reunion to watch a Marvel superhero movie and to relive our comic past. (We had spent most of our dorm days reading comics.) In the course of discussing our midlife crises, one asked me, "How do you keep motivated doing what you're doing?"

I chuckled and replied, "It's not hard to be motivated to do *nothing*," which is sort of how I see my work. With my teaching schedule, I have a lot of flexible, seemingly spare time. When others complain that I never am at work, I justify my apparent slothfulness: "I never rest. I'm always thinking."

In actuality, my mother has been a great model for how to stay motivated. Like her and like Father Pedro Arupe, the former Father General of the Society of Jesus, I see my vocational calling as being a "man for others."

I do not feel called to a specific vocation but I do feel summoned to pursue something much larger than my own individual goals, much more significant than my own personal destiny. This calling is to accept God's invitation to his party. This second sense of Christian calling, our royal bidding to be a part of God's people and to join in God's movement in the world, has been worth pursuing even despite our hardships.

Called to a New Hope

New Hope Covenant Church began when workers from two groups, Harbor House and Oak Park Ministries, recognized that they were discipling lots of young persons, but these individuals weren't joining local churches. They were low-income students of color who could not understand the language of the sermons at immigrant congregations, nor did they fit in at white, mainstream churches. Having grown up in Oakland, they had their own subculture of hip-hop and gangs, taco trucks and pho noodles, American pop culture and street English. They needed a place of their own where they could learn to follow Jesus in their setting, worship him with their ways of heartfelt expression, and develop as leaders without the dominating presence of outsiders. In ministering to our neighborhood, they were the ones who could reach out and share the gospel with their friends and families better than anyone else.

The experiences, attitudes, and language of these youth were so different from mine that I needed a translator to cross cultures. Once at a discipleship group for young men, we discussed the news of Oakland Police Department (OPD) SWAT activity in East Oakland. The boys spontaneously cheered when they heard that some OPD SWAT members got shot. I was shocked by their hardened attitudes and could barely understand them. They had become so resentful of the OPD's treatment of them that the OPD, as a whole, were seen as their enemies. They would never help the police, or even report crimes committed against themselves.

Another time, we watched a movie, *Mortal Combat,* based on a video game. The Chinese hero, Liu Kang, goes on a long pilgrimage in his dangerous quest to seek answers from the god of thunder, Raiden. After a tortuous journey, he finally reaches the summit of a high mountain. Entering a monastery through huge gates with a dragon insignia, Liu Kang is met by rows of shaven Asian monks in saffron robes kneeling and chanting. He strides through the incense wafting throughout the long, ancient chamber lined with hundreds of candles until he reaches another door to the throne room. The doors swing open on their own, and Liu Kang immediately bows and hides his eyes. When bidden, he looks up and finally meets the god, Raiden. Wearing a conical, bamboo hat, Raiden turns out to be a middle-aged white guy in a rice paddy uniform.

Spell-bound and hushed to this point, thirteen-year-old Samath cried out in disgust, "Man, God is always white!" The boys were very conscious of the racial hierarchy in Oakland and their segregation from white America. They only encountered one or two whites in high school because of the middle-class flight from Oakland public schools. Indeed, they were twice as likely to meet Pacific Islanders in their classes as to see Caucasians. When God is white—as American evangelical Christianity often presents him—then he becomes alien and foreign to our young men.

Locked out from jobs and access to the mainstream, the boys readily buy into oppositional culture that derides white, middle-class lifestyle. Their language, too, comes from the streets. At another meeting, I spoke about acting like Jesus—humble, without being pretentious. The guys stared at me numbly. Tane, the older brother-in-law of some of the guys, translated, "You don't be getting your shine on, y'know?" With this clarification, the guys nodded in agreement. Some people use the New International Version (NIV) of the Bible, but we need the New Urban Translation for Today's Youth (NUTTY) for our groups.

Our faith had to be translated, contextualized, and made real to these young Christians in the Murder Dubs. Strategies of the purposeful or emergent church, of emotionally healthy spirituality or inner healing, or of neo-Calvinism were not high on the list of concerns of our congregation. Instead, we needed to deal with friends who were being deported, alcoholic fathers who were abusive, and families who were being evicted due to foreclosures. Our members were single mothers whose boyfriends abandoned the family, young persons whose parents were absent due to wartime post-traumatic stress, and undocumented youth who could not find work without proper papers. In short, we served widows, orphans, and aliens—precisely those in the Bible whose interests we are to protect.[8]

Sadly, my elite education and even my evangelical Christian training did not equip me well to share the gospel with my neighbors in a relevant manner. Despite my shortcomings, I held to the vision that God wanted something much more for all of us in East Oakland than the struggles we faced. Along with other church founders, I longed that our young people, their friends, and their families might be called to hope in their difficult situations. We prayed for our young people just as Paul prayed for the Ephesians: "I pray that the eyes of your hearts may be enlightened in order that you may know the hope to which he has called you, the riches of his glorious inheritance in his holy people, and his incomparably great power for us who believe" (Eph. 1:18–19).[9]

This calling to a new hope is rich and powerful, particularly for those who are oppressed and exploited. In my own family history, I can see why certain groups grasped the good news found in Jesus. In Southern China, the Hakka were the ones who responded most to the missionaries in Guangdong Province. Being on the losing side of the

Taiping Rebellion and the Punti-Hakka Wars, they yearned for victory in Jesus. Joan's family in Korea became Christians during the Japanese occupation of that nation. When Japanese soldiers ordered the Koreans to bow to an image of the Japanese emperor, Joan's grandfather resolutely refused. Like many other Koreans, he stood for the promise of another kingdom. Long oppressed by the majority Burman government, Bethsy and Bonny's family converted along with their fellow Chin State people. Even when their churches were burned down by the Burmese army, they remained faithful to God's call.

The young people of Oakland are much like the Hakka in China, the Koreans under Japanese occupation, and the Chin in Burma. Similar to those in Corinth, not many minority youth in Oakland are "wise by human standards; not many were influential; not many were of noble birth" (1 Cor. 1:26).

In this status, they can respond more readily than those with privilege and power to God's invitation of grace. After all, Jesus himself said that it's hard for a rich man to enter the kingdom of heaven. Likewise, as I identify more as Hakka, I hear God's invitational call more clearly. For "God called the foolish things of the world to shame the wise; God chose the weak things of the world to shame the strong. God chose the lowly things of the world and the despised things . . ." (1 Cor. 1:27–28).

Called Out of Darkness into His Light

In being called to a new hope, we become God's church. As St. Peter explained, we are the church, *ekklesia*, "called . . . out of darkness into His marvelous light" (1 Peter 2:9 NASB). It also means that we are his holy assembly, called out of our homes by God to gather for his sacred purposes.[10]

One place where my family and I are called out to gather for holy purposes each Sunday is New Hope's Sacred Space, our corporate worship service. Sometimes during our services, people spend time at worship stations, where they have a range of opportunities to praise God in their individual and cultural expressions of faith. Some people pray before a globe for the world's needs. Others do graffiti art to express how they see God on the streets. Sometimes the *Oakland Tribune* newspaper is spread out, and we write prayers on sticky notes for the city. My favorite worship station is comprised of empty picture frames that focus our gazes outside a storefront window.

Sacred Space meets at the Youth Employment Partnership (YEP), a nonprofit agency on International Boulevard, one of the main streets running through the city. When we look out through those frames onto the streets, we catch a glimpse of the daily lives of our neighbors. Homeless people shuffle by, their carts loaded with recyclables. Elderly Asian immigrants in hand-knit hats and sweaters line up for distributions of free food. Mothers dressed in colorful, Guatemalan woven skirts carry their babies on their backs. As we watch them, we are moved to pray.

The more we watch, though, the more we see the darkness around us.

The people we see the most on our streets are women engaged in commercial sex work. International Boulevard is known as the Circuit, "the hub in the West for child prostitution," where pimps rotate individual women from city to city.[11] As crack sales declined in recent years, the selling of sex took over. The demand was higher, the overhead costs were less for the gangs, and the punishments were less severe. In our neighborhood, parents walking their children to school pass by groups of provocatively clad young women on every block of International Boulevard. Sadly, these scenes offer a warped sense of sexuality in which human bodies are cheapened and "the spirit of prostitution leads them astray" (Hosea 4:12). We fear that the prostitution draws sexual predators into our neighborhood. One semester, four local schools—including Matthew's—had attempted child assaults on their premises.[12]

Human trafficking on our streets has worsened. YEP's executive director observes that as soon as her male students get their paychecks and walk out the door, girls from the street offer their services, while pimps approach female YEP students and offer them higher earnings than what they just received. Pastor Dan, in response, felt called that our church should be there among the youth, offering some protection and surveillance. So his own small group meets at YEP every Friday night, and they organize Peace Walks once a month to pray over the streets.

One Friday night as the group met for a meal, a pregnant woman walked through the doors. From the way she was dressed, Dan could tell that she worked the streets. When the New Hope members invited her to join for dinner, she ravenously scarfed down the desserts. She spoke about not having a place to stay that night, but when they asked her more questions, she rambled incoherently because she was so strung out. At a loss about how to assist her, the group just sat and ate with her.

When the meal was finished, she walked back out onto International Boulevard and disappeared into nightfall. This encounter profoundly disturbed each member even though all had been in Oakland for decades. A week later, they still wondered what they should have done. One expressed his concern for this woman but was even more concerned for her unborn child. "What's our moral responsibility to keep that child safe?" he asked the group later. "Could we have the mother committed to a hospital to keep her from selling herself on the streets?"

We at New Hope are not alone in seeing sex trafficked on a daily basis. It seems like everywhere we look, on billboards and on bus stops, products are sold through sex. Because American corporate media has a monopoly over our cultural spaces, they market and advertise products everywhere to get us to sate our appetites. Throughout our society, the spirit of prostitution and consumerism is brazenly displayed.

New Hope, like other churches, is called out of this world to be salt and light. At times, as in the issue of sex trafficking, we can easily rally against the sin and develop compassion for the victims. For other issues, we in the middle class are so thoroughly enmeshed in our lifestyles of consumption and affluence that we are scarcely aware of our depravity, the spirit of prostitution, or others' suffering. We remain clueless about how we degrade God's creation or reduce others to great poverty. We are oblivious to staggering racial inequality in the United States that causes millions to be incarcerated or deported. This complicity is masked to us as we are caught up in the privileges of the American empire; we fail to recognize that, worldwide, more individuals today are displaced by war, violence, and poverty than at any time in history. Sadly, we are too busy to see the world for what it is.

Being called out of the world, then, requires the perspective of a stranger and foreigner, that of an exile and a Hakka. Hakka guest persons like Hall Gock Tie recognized that they did not fully fit into their societies but had different identities. This vision of a separate homeland enabled them to identify the faults of their host societies, whether that might be the violence of the Qing Dynasty or the racism of California. It also fueled them as they fought for shalom and justice; Hall Gock Tie sued for her rights and that of her fellow Chinese.

As a guest to this world, I can see enough of it to say that I do not want it. The spirit of prostitution in which children are bought and sold, the random violence that killed Jose, and the mindless non-compassion of society implicate all of us. I seek the peace of our city, but I yearn even more for Jesus to come. As we sing in the old African American spiritual, "You can have all the world, but give me Jesus."

Called Together as a New People

Our calling is not an individual one; it is a collective one to be God's new people. Peter sees God's elect—scattered as exiles—as "a chosen people, a royal priesthood, a holy nation, God's special possession" (1 Peter 2:9–10). Similarly, Paul writes that God's purpose in Jesus' sacrifice was "to create in himself one new humanity out of the two, thus making peace." Consequently, we are "fellow citizens with God's people and also members of his household" (Eph. 2:15, 19).

At New Hope, we take seriously our call to be God's new, reconciled people. We aim to be a multiracial and multiclass congregation because God has called us out from the world, including its categories and practices of oppression and domination. The stories of my Hakka great-grandmother and my mother, of the Oak Park families and the young women on the streets speak of the deep wounds and scars caused by racism, poverty, and sexism. We thus stand against the world's sin and its powerful effects.

As St. Paul wrote in three letters to churches in various cities, those adopted into God's family are seen as "neither Jew nor Gentile, neither slave nor free, nor is there male and female" (Gal. 3:28).[13] In Oakland, that reconciliation can be understood that in Jesus, we are neither "Latino nor African American, refugee nor high tech worker, nor is there straight and gay." We have equal status as saints, and together we are set apart for God's uses.

Although we reject the categories of the world that are used to oppress, we are still conscious of the power dynamics of race, class, and gender at New Hope. My experiences and perspective differ radically from Yien, the Mien grandmother who gardens in my backyard, or Carl, the African American young man who needed to stay at our apartment. As God redeems these categories and identities, he blesses us through the diversity of our backgrounds.

This unity and diversity are celebrated when God invites us to his party for prodigal sons and daughters each Sunday.

During Communion time at New Hope's Sacred Space, professional African Americans, working-class Southeast Asians, and middle-class whites stand up and join one of two lines. Just as all nations will stream to the mountain of the Lord's temple in the last days, we join one another when we are ready to receive Jesus' body and blood.[14] In doing so, we offer all that we are and have, including our cultural backgrounds and family heritages, to Jesus.

We bring all that we are to the table because Jesus has given us first every good and perfect gift. When we get to the front of the line, we come before a Communion table covered in a maroon tablecloth adorned with Southeast Asian elephant patterns of gold silk thread. Placed beside an orchid on the table is a platter of sticky rice and mango juice.

For Asians, rice is a symbol of life and health. Chinese greet each other with the phrase, "Have you eaten rice yet?" as an expression of concern. Mothers feed their sick children a bowl of rice porridge to provide comfort and as an offering of love. A meal without rice is not a meal, according to my Korean American father-in-law. Jesus may be viewed as our daily bread, but for Asians, he is the rice of life who provides strength and nourishment. Food is my love language, so when I meet God at Communion, sticky rice—broken for me—feeds and sustains my soul. Similarly, mango juice is a deep reminder of the sweet communion that I have with God and those around me.

After all have eaten, New Hope members stand in song. Alternating in Spanish and English, we praise,

> Tienes tanto amor y eres tan paciente
> Tu nombre es grande y tu corazón
> Porque eres bueno, seguiré cantando
> 10, 000 razones para adorar[15]

For those in the room whose first language is Spanish, these lyrics better express their spirits. I concentrate more on trying to pronounce the words correctly, but singing in another language makes me more mindful of the translated meaning.

We then lead into the prayers of the people, when we lift up personal concerns for work or health, neighborhood issues regarding violence or blight, and global troubles including unrest, war, and epidemic. Again, God uses this time and the wide-ranging issues to affect church members' hearts and to pull us outside of ourselves and our own preoccupations. In this Sacred Space, we are reoriented through worship, song, and prayer. The presider concludes with the benediction, "The kingdom of God is at hand, and is too big to be kept behind these four walls. Therefore, New Hope, go in peace to love and serve the Lord," and we are sent back onto International Boulevard and into East Oakland.

This snapshot of New Hope's Sacred Space service expresses who we are. On an average Sunday, we currently have about sixty-five adults and thirty-five children. Thirty are East Asian, ten are Filipino, fifteen are

Southeast Asian, twenty are Caucasian, twenty are Latino, and five are African American. (Many of us are mixed race, but I group us into racial categories that make us look more diverse.)

Instead of attempting to transcend or mute our varied backgrounds, we share them. That's why our Communion has Asian elements. That's why our songs include Spanish lyrics. Beyond superficial acknowledgement of each other's background, we actively bless each other with the gifts and the wisdom of each other's cultural and racial experiences. My stereotypes are shattered as I learn of how my roommate Carl overcame homelessness. My faith is enriched as I receive prayer from Yien and hear of her victories over the spirit world. Sylvia's courage to stand up to deportation authorities shows me how to take positions of justice. Like every gift from God, our cultures are meant to be a blessing to others.

So we celebrate God with our cultures at New Hope. We would incorporate more hip-hop, but at this point, most of us look lame trying to move and rap to a mixed beat.

Our hip-hop ineptitude shows that we do have limitations as a congregation as we try to combine people of different backgrounds and perspectives. But the fact is that being a multicultural church is much easier than being a multiclass one. When we study Scripture or need sermon applications, the differences between economic backgrounds are often starkly revealed.

I recall that at one small group meeting, we each had to answer the icebreaker question, "What would you do differently in high school now that you know better?" Two women who are physicians, one from Stanford and another from Harvard, immediately responded, "I wouldn't have studied so much. There's so much more to life than books." In contrast, another woman expressed, "I would have studied harder to stay in school." The next stated, "Yeah, I wish I didn't play around so much and hadn't gotten pregnant." There was an awkward pause, and none of us looked at each other. Seemingly for the first time, the high school nerds were in the same room as the gangsters.

Unfortunately, at New Hope cliques can form along economic lines. Our social class shapes our experiences so much that those living just a zip code apart have radically different lifestyles, worldviews, and opportunities.[16]

Given our human tendency to stick with those like ourselves, the collective summons to be unified as the body of Christ is sounded again and again in the New Testament. We are urged to walk in a manner worthy of this calling as Christ's one body. Peter insists that we "make every effort to confirm" our calling of oneness (2 Peter 1:10). Because the divide between the rich and the poor was so wide in the church at Corinth, Paul instructed them to examine themselves before taking Communion and discern whether the body of Christ was acting in unity or not (1 Cor. 11:27–29).

As stated before, this calling is like a wedding invitation. At Chinese banquets, guests sit around circular tables so that there is no head of the table or need to pass dishes to those who cannot reach them. Instead, we all have equal access to the plates of food, which are placed on a rotating lazy Susan. Despite the fact that each guest can serve himself, my father always reminded me to serve those around me first. This unity at the banqueting table—along with the practices of equality and servanthood—aptly represents our Christian call to be one people, one church.

Called to Jesus

The amazing invitation from God—toward a new hope, out of darkness, and together as one—ultimately leads us to Jesus. In our identification with him, we come to know the extent of his suffering for us and, consequently, the magnitude of his love.

In his letters, Peter wrote to the Christian exiles of Asia Minor who had to "suffer grief in all kinds of trials" (1 Peter 1:6) and explained that we are called to follow Christ's example of suffering (2:21). The trials in that time may have included social discrimination and being reviled, or official persecution and mass executions of Christians by the Roman Empire. Today, however, we Americans do not expect such kinds of trials and suffering, which seem antithetical to our unalienable rights to "life, liberty, and the pursuit of happiness."

Instead, we feel entitled to happiness, and expect that God will grant it to us if we are faithful. In 2006, the cover of *Time* magazine featured a picture of a Rolls Royce with a cross as its hood ornament and asked, "Does God Want You To Be Rich?"[17] In the article's poll, a full 61 percent of American Christians responded, "Yes." Correspondingly high numbers believe that God will grant health to those who have enough faith. According to Kate Bowler, professor at Duke Divinity School, they learn such beliefs from church, where fifty of the 260 largest American megachurches preach the prosperity gospel and positive thinking.[18]

I believe that God showers us with good gifts and blesses us with the incomparable riches of heaven. At the same time, we are not to be surprised at suffering in this fallen world, for that is the lot for those who love.

Joan and I delight in and love having Matthew as our son; he brings us a sublime joy that is also bittersweet. When I watch him play with Legos, I want to hold onto and relish those moments. His nearness and joy at play bring to me a sense of overriding shalom, a peace that derives from wholeness and well-being. My heart also aches, though, because I am well aware of the evanescent nature of this joy. The moment will pass; Matthew will grow and change, and my cuddly son will all-too-soon be grown up.

The Japanese must have a word or phrase for this mixture of feelings, of joy and heartache. Just as they know that in the spring, cherry trees bloom with exquisite and fragile blossoms, they are also cognizant that these petals will presently flutter away in the breeze. I love and ache over Matthew with this type of awareness.

Unsurprisingly, then, Joan and I tried to have more children. After a few years without success, we began trying a variety of strategies, including both Western and Eastern medicines. Joan took hormones for months, risking her own health so that we could have a child. Our house reeked from Chinese herbal teas that we steeped in earthenware pots and drank to make us fertile. We had our skin pricked with smoking needles by acupuncturists so that our bodies might become more balanced. Once, Joan did conceive, and I skipped through a stream at Redwood Park singing the doxology out loud in crazed exultation. However, after only five weeks, we experienced a miscarriage.

We prayed and hoped for another chance despite our advancing ages. Then, Joan became pregnant again! We dared not get too optimistic, though, given our history.

A few weeks later, we were to attend a New Hope church retreat. Joan had begun to bleed as she had in previous pregnancies, so we faced the weekend with dread and anxiety. Would our long awaited baby survive to term?

Joan was leading worship for our congregation when she began to sense more bleeding.

I also was forebodingly desperate. I couldn't concentrate as our church studied the biblical passage of Jesus feeding the five thousand. In this story, of the five thousand present, Jesus' disciples could find only one young boy willing to give to Jesus. All he had to offer were his five small loaves of bread and two small fish.

In the chapel, I wept and wrestled with God about what I was being asked to give up. My five small loaves were our five years dreaming of and trying to have another child to complete our family. My two small fish were the two babies—sweet little girls, I'm sure—that would never see the light of day.

Later that day, I broke my hip in a freak fall. With any movement, I gasped in excruciating pain due to the fracture. I later found out that before anesthesia, people with such an injury were often left to die because they could not be moved.[19] I underwent immediate surgery to have pins inserted in my femur.

I awoke after the operation, and I learned that Joan had once again miscarried.

When I arrived home after that terrible weekend, our short flight of stairs was too high for me to climb. I couldn't lift my legs, so I faltered midway, letting out an anguished moan. Literally and symbolically, I was stopped in my tracks. My greatest yearning, the ineffable joy of being a father once again, was lost.

Suffering, whether it be the love-ache of evanescent moments or the grief over lost children, is part and parcel of our human condition. It comes with the package of loving. What boggles my mind is that God of heaven came in the form of Jesus to also endure this condition. I may have given my five small loaves and two small fish, but he offered up so much more.

I cannot hazard to make sense out of suffering, but I do recognize that Jesus' co-suffering with us is a mark of his compassion and love. My aching finds its source from my love for Matthew and my grieving is over my lost relationship with our unborn babies. God's sufferings as a human is a result, too, of his love for us as his children. Though some Christians expect health and wealth, I know now that suffering and lament are inevitable parts of our Christian journey. It is part of our call to be like Jesus, to have a loving heart open to the joys and sorrows of others.

Paul wanted to know Christ, especially the power of his resurrection and the fellowship of his sufferings (Phil. 3:10). Most of us desire that power, but we avoid the suffering. Paul, I think, participates in Christ's sufferings so that he can understand the full extent of God's love.

At Home in Exile

My story closes with Jose's tragic death and all the unanswered questions it raises. Jose gave up everything to minister to those on the margins. But I'm privileged and professional. I want my family to be safe and comfortable. Am I really to be like the rich young ruler and like Jose, called to give up everything—my career and my family dreams—to follow Jesus?

202 At Home in Exile

Jose's passing brings to the fore not just questions for myself, but also vexing dilemmas for our church. How do we collectively respond to the senseless violence and trauma we witness regularly? Our church conflict in the midst of his passing, in hindsight, seemed inevitable, and it remains very much a live issue for me. I wonder, how can the people of God overcome our own self-interests and work unceasingly for God's shalom? Will we ever see lasting, concrete change in ourselves and in our society?

These questions of ministry and family life, of church and justice, continue to perplex and even haunt me. I don't have the full answers to any of them, but I do have something: God has given me a calling that grounds me and points the way.

Peter reminds us that we followers of Jesus are "foreigners and exiles" (1 Peter 2:11). Although temporarily banished in this corrupt world, we don't belong nor should we try to belong to it as it is. Instead, we have a different community; we are "citizens with God's people and also members of his household" (Eph. 2:19). Soon and very soon, we can expect Jesus to come again so that his reign of peace and justice, of love and mercy, will prevail.

Quite literally then, God calls us to be guest families who recognize that we do not fit in this world, and that our present sufferings will soon pass. This knowledge enables us to endure and hope. It frees us to travel through this life lightly while, at the same time, resolutely seeking the peace of the city. In fact, the Hakka were described as "a people of the future" precisely because they could suffer through forced migration time and time again as they diligently worked for a real home.

And today, we Christians in the United States are continually invited by the King of Kings to a rich and royal calling. God invites us to be Hakka.

Just like my great-grandmother, Hall Gock Tie, we may never receive a "special" calling and find some great, passionate work. Rather, we may be simply ordinary folk who toil to take care of ourselves and others. Similar to other Hakka, we may never feel fully "at home" here on this earth. Instead, we're much more likely to face suffering and lamentations, especially if we love deeply.

Nevertheless, being guests, we can find comfort in one thing: We remain guests of the King, invited and called to be at home in exile.

Epilogue

A few years ago, I wrote out my bucket list, which included all the things I wanted to accomplish by my fiftieth birthday. The one major item that I definitely wanted to check off was to complete a 50K trail race. Being able to call myself an "ultramarathoner" sounded cool, so I trained and persisted. Eventually, even though I felt like Frodo climbing to Mordor, I completed the run. Despite coming in third from last and having some really old, large runners beat me, I was quite pleased with myself.

The next day, Joan and I met with some refugees from Bhutan to help them do a needs assessment. She proudly told Tek, who was staring at me because of how stiffly I moved, that I had just completed a long race in the steep hills by the Golden Gate Bridge.

"Ah," Tek intoned quietly. "I know what it is like, to run through mountains."

Immediately I felt chastened. I had run through the scenic Marin Headlands. He had run to cross the storming Himalayas. I wore ASICS gel shoes with biomorphic material for forefoot flexibility. He had hand-sewn sandals. I traveled lightly because volunteers provided electrolyte drinks and energy bars every five miles. He traveled lightly, carrying all his possessions. I ran in retreat from my world, to add to my bucket of experiences. He ran for his life.

I should have realized that my personal bucket list was vainglory. Fortunately, my neighbors—refugees from Cambodia, Laos, Bhutan, and Burma—daily instruct me on how I should live, as an exile in this world. And as I reclaim my Chinese Hakka heritage and seek solidarity with the poor, I too am receiving the blessings of being a guest in exile.

The Church in Exile

I have always been on the margins of the American evangelical subculture, so not until just recently have I become cognizant of evangelicalism's steep decline in adherence and influence. This shift may or may not signal the secularization of the United States. It does, however, demonstrate how the American church is a church in exile.

In the fall of 2014, I spoke at eight evangelical Christian universities and seminaries across the nation. At each, the administration confided concerns about their enrollment numbers and thoughts on how they direly needed to rethink the role of theological education. Fewer individuals than before are considering full-time ministry as pastors, and those who do attend seminary plan to enter different types of work. Since the all-time peak enrollment at seminaries in 2006, the number of students seeking a master's degree in divinity declined 7.6 percent by 2013.[1]

These new ministers will face a shrinking job market as church attendance drops. Overall, church attendance has dropped 7 percent in the last decade, and the number of those who attend church regularly has also dipped.[2] The mainline church has experienced this drop for the past few decades, but now evangelicals also are witnessing this alarming downward shift. Startlingly, one in four Southern Baptist churches reported no baptisms in 2014; indeed, 60 percent stated that they hadn't baptized any youth, so prospects for the future appear dim.[3]

Evangelicals also must deal with their waning influence in the public square. One example is at my own university, San Francisco State University. In 2011, all twenty-three California State University (CSU) campuses—the nation's largest university system—implemented a nondiscrimination policy regarding student leadership of campus organizations. InterVarsity Christian Fellowship (IVCF), however, wanted its leaders to continue to affirm its doctrinal statement. Rather than acceding to the state policy, this national organization chose to lose campus recognition as an official student group.[4] Without this recognition, they had to use guerilla tactics to find meeting space on campus. Whenever they found an open spot, they would text the other members to gather.

In the war between multicultural tolerance and religious freedom, it seemed that tolerance had won this battle. This evangelical organization gave up school recognition so that they could maintain the integrity of their faith. Since they saw the policy as part of a larger intellectual trend against religious freedom, they felt that they had to draw a line in the sand. Eventually, the CSU worked out a compromise agreement and InterVarsity is an official organization again.

American evangelicals, perhaps too self-confident in their own privilege and power, must recognize that their influence, especially among millennials, is waning rapidly. American society is no longer Christian—if it ever was. Instead, the church is in exile, a minority group no longer fully at home in the United States. And rather than being too cozy in this world, I maintain, that's a good place to be.

Lessons from My People and Other Exiles

As my pitiful need to check off items on my bucket list indicates, I am typically American in my individualism. I need to consume experiences in order to be fulfilled.

Fortunately, reclaiming the stories of my family and learning from my Chinese background helps to reorient me from my self-obsessed perspective. This history connects me to the hardships of others so that I can relate and empathize. Through my great-grandmother, Hall Gock Tie, I can feel for those who have had to flee war and resettle in new lands, only to be displaced again. From my grandfather, Hop Shue, I see the devastating effects of undocumented status and racial segregation, and I can still feel the wounds of Orientalism today. My mother's own experiences with the foster care system illustrate the tragedy of public policies and how they rip apart families. When I see the racialized effects of our American policies of mass incarceration and deportation, I weep because my own family, as people of color, experienced similar injustices. For me, these family stories are integral to learning how to be a gracious guest and an exiled foreigner.

As a guest person, I am at the mercy of my hosts. This dependency and reliance upon others helps to sever me from my American self-sufficiency. In American ministries, we often prefer to arrive with grand strategies and deep pockets. When I moved to Oak Park, though, the table was turned as I became the guest of the poor and a recipient from refugees. These people of peace generously granted me succor and protection as I lived among them. Individuals—such as Carl Williams, Veasna Ourm, and Sylvia Lopez—welcomed me to Oakland. Through the years, they've shown me that the fruit of righteousness is God's shalom—his deep, thoroughgoing peace with him and others.

We may get a taste of peace, but sooner or later, we will hunger and thirst for righteousness again as exiles. Over the twenty-plus years that I have lived at Oak Park and in the Murder Dubs, the pernicious consequences of personal and systemic sin have been ever-present. The easy money from the sale of drugs in our parking lot is now obtained through the sale of sex at our front door. The violence of gang-banging continues as gunshots over our house are often heard throughout the night. The lines for free food giveaways down the block are multiethnic; people hungry for food come from all parts of the world. The San Francisco Bay Area has been gentrified at an unprecedented rate, but our neighborhood remains graffitied and strewn with dumped garbage at every corner.

As a Chinese American, I view this need for righteousness and justice through a collective lens. Justice is more than the securement of individual rights. It also encompasses the equitable and substantive distribution of resources that enhances the community's well-being. Our struggles for justice at Oak Park—battles against racial profiling, for basic welfare safety nets, and for decent housing—were enactments of our responsibility for the common good, and especially for the marginalized and weak.

And yet. Even when we won our housing settlement at Oak Park, we didn't get to live happily ever after. Unintentionally, we lost our sense of community. As Pastor Dan states, "We'd like to say we won the lawsuit and lived happily ever after, but we can't. We did win, and it was a good chapter in our story. But the story and the struggle continue."

How do we Christians persist despite being part of an empire that exploits and oppresses the poor? What keeps us going when our societal problems seem insurmountable and little appears to change?

Again, I must take lessons from the Hakka people and our fellow exiles.

Life as Exiles

I may have chosen to live at Oak Park and in East Oakland, but I couldn't expect my wife and family to stay there also. After all, immigrant families move to this nation for a better life, so it seems contradictory—dishonoring even, to the immigrant parents—to choose to dwell among the underclass.

Fortunately, I met Joan, who shares my call to meet Jesus among the poor. As our relationship progressed, I recognized how our Asian perspective shaped how our family relates. My love language is different from what is spoken in American television sitcoms or in Christian marriage books. It is based on a loyal love—like God's *hesed* relationship with his church bride—that assumes a permanent, covenantal relationship. Joan and I share that loyal love, even if she does seem like an international student to me with her circular and indirect communication style. And, even despite the basic flaws in my character, she puts up with me. This faithfulness wouldn't make for a great romantic comedy, but it makes for a strong marriage.

Raising a family in the ghetto has been difficult for us, especially when we consider the safety and education of our children. In one of his fourth-grade school essays, Matthew wrote that the one thing he would change about our neighborhood is its lack of safety. He explained, "In my neighborhood, it is unsafe, beaten up, and poor. There are many things I would like to be changed, but safety is the largest aspect I would like to see amended. Currently, I am not allowed out onto the street ever without an adult, and people need another person with them to go out at night. Insecurity dampens my community, but I believe if it were safer, it would thrive." I know why we have an obesity epidemic among America's low-income children. Parents, like me, don't feel safe letting them go out to play and exercise.

Overall, Joan and I do our best to protect our children, and we have the gift of our church community to help us do so. Some focus on the family to nurture healthy self-esteem and to establish independent persons. Others, such as Tiger parents, instill strict discipline in order to develop high-achieving individuals. Along with aiming to raise confident, independent, and high-achieving children, Joan and I also view our family as part of a larger family, to whom and for whom we are responsible. We seek to impart to our children a character of compassion, not competitiveness. We want to inculcate a value for interdependence, not self-dependence. Our community may not be the safest place to raise children, but it's a great context in which to develop the values of the Beatitudes. We really do believe that "blessed are the poor," "blessed are those who hunger and thirst," and "blessed are the peacemakers." That's why we remain in our community. That's what we teach our children.

The Chinese value for interdependence, in turn, influences how I see work. I would like my work to be a personal calling where my potential is realized and where my core values are expressed. That ideal privilege, though, is limited to a select few. Most of us—like my mother, Bernice—work for utilitarian ends to take care of our family; that in itself should be seen as noble and significant. Indeed, we should fight for workers' rights and immigration reform so that everyone is able to work and take care of their families well.

As much as I would like an individualized calling to feel special and important, we Christians have been invited to a much larger purpose. Our primary calling is to be the church called by God, to God, and for God.[5] A Hakka worldview deepens my love for the church. As landless immigrants seeking a new home, my ancestors had a distinct perspective on California. They settled here, raised families, and sought the peace of the community. Yet they never were accepted. Instead, my great-grandparents and their community had to sue for justice again and again. Similarly, the church—in light of its exile and especially because of its exile—should call people out of darkness and into a new hope of a different world. It should be called together as a reconciled, new people who are particularly united through Jesus. Although the church may not be fully accepted, it can still be a blessing to others and society.

As a united and reconciled body, the church can reject the ways of oppression and the use of race, class, and gender that the world employs to divide people. By suffering alongside others, American Christians can demonstrate the compassion and grace already granted to us by God. The church as an institution may have its frailties, but the church as the family of God is his instrument of peace.

Guests of the King, Love Languages of the Kingdom

Our struggles at my home church and in our neighborhood continue. Individuals leave our congregation because of conflicts or trials, the same issues that the early church confronted. Racial hostilities and class inequalities continue to grow, leaving us angry and dispirited. However, Peter and Paul wrote that these difficulties are not new. We should expect them, because we are foreigners and exiles in a world with a different set of allegiances.

We can endure our momentary difficulties because Christians have a new citizenship—belonging to heaven and seeing themselves as heirs of the kingdom. We act as citizens of heaven now by caring for others with the same mutual responsibility with which Asians express love. Asian parents are willing to sacrifice everything—especially their hard work and careers—for their family. Their children see this sacrifice and respond through their own work ethic and gifts of honor. That's one of the reasons why Asian immigrant children work so hard at school. We should respond to Jesus' sacrifice for us in a similar way. Recognizing his gifts, we should want to offer all of our efforts in response. So even though we face suffering and setbacks, we continue to love with a deep reservoir of grace.

I understand Jesus' sacrifice the most and feel most worshipful when I receive Communion. In the tangible form of bread and wine, I receive God's gifts. I knew my father loved me when he would proudly take me out to eat at fine restaurants. I feel cared for when my mother cracks crab legs for me because she knows I love the meat but am too lazy to dig it out myself. God feeds me, too. Every week when New Hope celebrates the Eucharist, I enjoy a full banquet and am filled with just a piece of bread and a little juice.

These love languages—through sacrifice and food—are how I receive God's devoted love, even when circumstances of the world dictate otherwise.

Honored at Home in Exile

Ultimately, God is making us a home, where he will host us as his guests and children. This honor at a party, as exemplified in the Prodigal Son (Luke 15:11–32), brings me to my final thought about being at home in exile.

My neighbors and my daughters dislike being called "refugees." They are disturbed by the stereotype of refugees as poor and hapless. Not surprisingly, they are ashamed of being displaced and without a home. As an Asian American, I can understand the deep sense of shame that a lot of Asians feel. I am very conscious of how others see me, and if I do lose face, I want to run away and hide.

The Bible also talks about shame. It addresses this topic much more than it discusses the Western notion of guilt, because Jesus lived in a shame-based culture. For every time guilt is mentioned in the Bible, shame is addressed three times as often.[6] So Jesus' sacrifice not only deals with our guilt, but God also addresses the shame of our sin. While shame drives us away from God in embarrassment and fear, the death of Jesus reconciles us to him and restores our honor.

This Asian view of salvation—that God rescues me from both my guilt *and* my shame—has revived my worship, such that I often weep upon taking Communion. I love singing about how God has brought me out of darkness and hiding into his marvelous light; about how I am unworthy, but he makes me blameless and pure; and that my shame is gone, and now I am honored as his child.

When Matthew was born, we gave him a Chinese name, "Zhang Guan Hui." Translated, his name is "crown of glory" and comes from Isaiah 61. Instead of the crown of ashes that exiles wear to display their shame, God will give us a crown of beauty and glory—"a planting for his splendor." Matthew's preciousness and worth, like all of ours, is derived from the honor with which God graces us.

I've always wanted to be special and unique in this world. What I've learned from my family and gained from my refugee neighbors is a more precious gift. I have come to realize that both now and in the future, each of us is honored as a guest of the King. Even despite our temporary sufferings, in the midst of this fallen world, and in light of our shame, God knows our yearnings. And given his loyal love and his overwhelming peace, all of us—refugees, foreigners, aliens, and strangers—can learn to be at home in exile.

Notes

Chapter 1: Welcomed as a Guest

1. Mao Tse-Tung, *Quotation from Chairman Mao Tse-Tung* (San Francisco: China Books and Periodicals, 2008), 170.
2. Martin Luther King Jr., *Letter from Birmingham Jail* (April 16, 1963). See, for example, *Atlantic Monthly*, vol. 212, no. 2 (August 1963): 78-88.
3. Some names in this memoir have been changed to maintain anonymity and confidentiality.
4. The interpretation that Jesus' miracle was to help people share is open for debate. What I want to stress is how our neighbors' circumstances shaped their reading of the Bible, as do the circumstances of readers with other class backgrounds shape theirs. See Ernesto Cardenal, *The Gospel in Solentiname* (Maryknoll, NY: Orbis Press, 1976).
5. Robert Bellah, Richard Madsen, William M. Sullivan, Ann Swidler, and Steven M. Tipton, *Habits of the Heart: Individualism and Commitment in American Life* (Berkeley: University of California Press, 2007).
6. M. Scott Peck, *The Different Drum: Community Making and Peace* (New York: Simon & Schuster, 1987).
7. 1 Corinthians 11 challenges Christians to examine themselves before taking Communion to see if they are living out the unity created by Christ.

Chapter 2: Ancestral Choices

1. This "best-selling" attribute is from *Publishers Weekly* and the *New York Times*.
2. Rick Warren, *The Purpose Driven Life: What on Earth Am I Here For?* (Grand Rapids: Zondervan, 2002), 248.
3. E. J. Eitel, "Ethnographic Sketches of the Hakka Chinese," *Notes and Queries on China and Japan* 7 (1867): 81.
4. These accounts of the Chinese at Point Alones can be found in Sandy Lydon's excellent book *Chinese Gold: The Chinese in Monterey Bay Region* (Capitola, CA: Capitola Book Co., 1985).
5. Song written and composed by television director and producer Paul Henning, 1962.
6. Ralph Ellison, *The Invisible Man* (London: Vintage, 1952), page unknown.

Chapter 3: Guests and Hosts of People of Peace

1. Andy Crouch, *Culture Making: Recovering Our Creative Calling* (Downers Grove, IL: InterVarsity Presss, 2013).
2. Tim Keller, *Center Church: Doing Balanced, Gospel-Centered Ministry in Your City* (Grand Rapids: Zondervan, 2012), 150.
3. Ibid., 146.
4. Stanley Hauerwaus and William Willimon, *Resident Aliens: Life in the Christian Colony* (Nashville: Abingdon Press, 2014); John Perkins, *Restoring At-Risk Communities: Doing It Together and Doing It Right* (Grand Rapids: Baker Books, 1995).

Chapter 4: An Asian American Dream for Justice

1. Gary A. Haugen, *Good News About Injustice: A Witness of Courage in a Hurting World*, 10th Anniversary. Ed. (Downers Grove, IL: InterVarsity Press, 2009), 86.
2. Dennis Jacobsen, *Doing Justice: Congregations and Community Organizing* (Minneapolis: Fortress Press, 2004), 54.

3. Zhu Ningzhu, "China Hits Back with Report on U.S. Human Rights Record," *Xinhua Net* (April 21, 2013).

4. *The Analects of Confucius* 1:6.

5. *Mishpat,* the Hebrew term for justice, includes both procedural fairness and equitable social relations. Walter Bruggemann describes shalom as "an enduring Sabbath of joy and well-being." See Walter Bruggemann, *Peace: Understanding Biblical Themes* (St. Louis: Chalice Press, 2001), 18.

6. Tim Golden, "If Immigrants Lose U.S. Aid, Local Budgets May Feel Pain," *New York Times* (July 29, 1996).

7. Lynn Fujiwara, *Mothers Without Citizenship: Asian Immigrant Families and the Consequences of Welfare Reform* (Minneapolis: University of Minnesota Press, 2008), 20.

8. William Wong, "Fears of Falling with a Shrinking Safety Net Below," *Oakland Tribune* (December 18, 1995).

9. Barbara Nicholson, "The Influence of Pre-Emigration and Postemigration Stressors on Mental Health: A Study of Southeast Asian Refugees," *Social Work Research* 21, no. 1: 19-31 (1997).

10. An article from the *San Francisco Chronicle* pictured Oak Park as an example of California's environmental crisis exacerbated by the inflow of immigrants. See Harold Gilliam, "Bursting at the Seams: California's Immigration Crisis," *San Francisco Chronicle* (February 21, 1993).

11. Laura Counts, "A Clean Fight: Shabby Building Spurs Formation of Unlikely Tenants Association," *Oakland Tribune* (April 19, 1999).

12. Libby Schaaf went on to become a city council member and in 2014 was elected mayor of Oakland.

13. Janine DeFao, "New Attack on Oakland Slumlords: City Levies Fines, Disgruntled Renters Sue," *San Francisco Chronicle* (October 29, 1999).

14. Andy Crouch, *Playing God: Rdeeming the Gift of Power* (Downers Grove, IL: InterVarsity Books, 2013), 220.

15. Stanley Hauerwaus and William Willimon, *Resident Aliens: Life in the Christian Colony* (Nashville: Abingdon Press, 2014), 38.

16. See Hebrews 11:14-16.

Chapter 5: Tiger Moms, Teddy Bear Dads, and a Panda Father

1. Laurence Steinberg and Anne Levine, *You and Your Adolescent: The Essential Guide for Ages 10-25* (New York: Simon & Schuster, 1997).

2. "Be perfect, therefore, as your heavenly Father is perfect" (Matt. 5:48).

3. In a 2009 national survey, the Committee of 100, a civil rights organization, found that a high percentage (45 percent) of Americans suspect that Chinese Americans are more loyal to China in military or economic conflicts than to the U.S. *US-China Public Perceptions Opinion Survey 2012.* http://survey.committee100.org/2012/2012survey.php?lang=en&p=1&q=1 (accessed June 9, 2014).

4. Focus on the Family is one such well-known evangelical group. It has this laudable aim: "We provide help and resources for couples to build healthy marriages that reflect God's design, and for parents to raise their children according to morals and values grounded in biblical principles." "About Focus on the Family." http://www.focusonthefamily.com/about_us.aspx (accessed June 4, 2014).

5. First published in 1995, the *Five Love Languages* remained on the top of Amazon's Christian Best-Seller Books for Marriage as of the summer of 2014. Gary Chapman, *The Five Love Languages: The Secret to Love That Lasts* (Chicago: Northfield Publishing, 2009).

6. Stephen Kendrick and Alex Kendrick, *The Love Dare.* (Nashville: B & H Publishing, 2008). This book is based on the film *Fireproof,* about one couple's marriage. This movie was the highest grossing independent film in 2008, and the book spent over 130 weeks on the *New York Times* best-sellers list.

7. Ibid., 38.

8. Henry Cloud and John Townsend, *Boundaries: When to Say Yes, When to Say No* (Grand Rapids: Zondervan, 1992).

9. According to the Love and Logic website, the authors' parenting approach helps "by being a trusted leader in the market for 35 years." If it doesn't work, they offer a money-back guarantee. http://www.loveandlogic.com/t-Why-Choose-Love-and-Logic-Programs.aspx (accessed June 16, 2014).

10. Foster Cline and Jim Fay, *Parenting with Love and Logic* (Colorado Springs: Navpress, 2006), 14.

11. Ibid., 243.

12. One Christian author wrote that the American premise for marriage is all wrong, and therefore our dissatisfaction with each other and our unfulfilled expectations are misplaced. Marriage isn't supposed to make us happy, but holy. Gary Thomas, *Sacred Marriage: What If God Designed Marriage to Make Us Holy More Than to Make Us Happy* (Grand Rapids: Zondervan, 2000).

13. Sam Ro, "A Third of America's 18-to-34 Year Olds Live with Their Parents," *Business Insider* (June 2, 2014).

14. Yosemite posts warning signs about bears everywhere, and we read that bears are attracted especially to minivans, since they tend to have car seats with lots of food trapped underneath them. See Peter Fimrite, "Hungry Yosemite Bears Zero In on Minivans," *San Francisco Chronicle* (October 24, 2009).

15. Hilary Abramson, "Christian Activists Show Faith in East Oakland," *San Francisco Chronicle* (September 20, 2010).

16. Evan Sernoffsky, "Oakland's Public Face Pockmarked with Graffiti," *San Francisco Chronicle* (June 5, 2014).

17. S. Robers, J. Zhang, and J. Truman, *Indicators of School Crime and Safety* (Washington, DC: National Center for Education Statistics, U.S. Department of Education; and Bureau of Justice Statistics, Office of Justice Programs, U.S. Department of Justice, 2010).

18. 1 Peter 4:8 says, "Above all, love each other deeply, because love covers over a multitude of sins."

19. In Oakland, student assignment at a school is made by lottery. First priority goes to those who live in a school's proximity, and second priority is for those with siblings already at the school. Third priority in assignment is for those whose local schools have low scores in standardized tests. These families have the option of sending their children outside their neighborhood school zone.

20. In contrast, Jesus commanded, "Seek first [God's] kingdom and his righteousness, and all these things will be given to you as well" (Matt. 6:33).

21. Alexia Salvatierra and Peter Heitzel, *Faith-Rooted Organizing: Mobilizing the Church in Service to the World* (Downers Grove, IL: InterVarsity Press, 2014).

22. Shoshana Walter, "Shootings Soar in Oakland; Children Often the Victims," *New York Times* (January 7, 2012).

23. "Only be careful, and watch yourselves closely so that you do not forget the things your eyes have seen or let them fade from your heart as long as you live. Teach them to your children and to their children after them. Remember the day you stood before the Lord your God at Horeb, when he said to me, 'Assemble the people before me to hear my words so that they may learn to revere me as long as they live in the land and may teach them to their children'" (Deut. 4:9-10).

Chapter 6: The Call as the Church in Exile

1. Richard N. Bolles, *What Color Is Your Parachute? A Practical Manual for Job-Hunters and Career-Changers* (New York: Ten Speed Press, revised annually).

2. Gordon T. Smith, *Courage and Calling: Embracing Your God-Given Potential* (Downers Grove, IL: InterVarsity Press, 2011).

3. Parker Palmer, *Let Your Life Speak: Listening for the Voice of Vocation* (San Francisco: Jossey-Bass, 2009).

4. Amy Sherman, *Kingdom Calling: Vocational Stewardship for the Common Good* (Downers Grove, IL: InterVarsity Press, 2011), 107.

5. Similarly, God commands that we are to work to support our family (1 Tim. 5:4). Before his death, Jesus made sure that his mother was cared for by John (John 19:26).

6. In Genesis 2, God gave Adam the creative work to give names to animals.

7. Isaiah 65:22 says, "No longer will they build houses and others live in them, or plant and others eat. For as the days of a tree, so will be the days of my people; my chosen ones will long enjoy the work of their hands."

8. See Malachi 3:5.

9. Other passages in which we are called to a future hope in heaven include Ephesians 4:4; Philippians 3:14; and Hebrews 3:1.

10. See Matthew 16:18 and Acts 2:47.

11. Katy Steinmetz, "Oakland Launches Pimp-Shaming Website," *Time* (July 2, 2014). http://time.com/2946597/oakland-launches-pimp -shaming-website/ (accessed July 18, 2014).

12. Kristin Bender, "Oakland Marchers Rally Against Recent Rash of Child Assaults," *Oakland Tribune* (April 10, 2014). http://www .insidebayarea.com/News/ci_25534120/Oakland-marchers-rally -against-recent-rash (accessed July 18, 2014).

13. See also 1 Corinthians 12:13 and Colossians 3:11.

14. See Isaiah 2:2.

15. "You're rich in love, and You're slow to anger. Your name is great, and Your heart is kind. For all Your goodness I will keep on singing. Ten thousand reasons for my heart to love." *Copyright © 2000-2016 AZLyrics.com*

16. Families living in two zip code areas away from Oak Park live six years longer, on average, than us. http://www.healthhappensinca.org/ (accessed July 25, 2014).

17. David Van Biesma and Jeff Chu, "Does God Want You to be Rich?" *Time* (September 6, 2006).

18. Kate Bowler, *Blessed: A History of the American Prosperity Gospel* (New York: Oxford University Press, 2013).

19. Even in 2014, American males over fifty years old had an eightfold risk of mortality three months after a hip fracture.

Epilogue

1. Leslie Scanlon, "Pathways to Seminary: New Report Highlights Seminary Enrollment Trends," *The Presbyterian Outlook* (September 18, 2013).

2. The Barna Group, "Americans Divided on the Importance of Church" (March 25, 2014). https://www.barna.org/barna-update/culture/661 -americans-divided-on-the-importance-of-church#.VJCK03vkdkk (accessed December 16, 2014).

3. Adelle Banks, "Southern Baptists Meet As Membership, Baptism Decline Continues," *Religious News Service* (June 4, 2014).

4. Carla Rivera, "Christian Group Fights for Identity Against Cal

State Policy," *Los Angeles Times* (October 29, 2014; Michael Paulson, "Colleges and Evangelicals Collide on Bias Policy," *New York Times* (June 9, 2014).

5. Os Guinness neatly summarizes that "Our primary calling as followers of Christ is by him, to him, and for him." Os Guinness, *The Call: Finding and Fulfilling the Central Purpose of Your Life* (Nashville: Word Publishing, 1998), 31.

6. Simon Chan, *Grassroots Asian Theology* (Downers Grove, IL: InterVarsity Press, 2014).